FEARLESS LEADERSHIP

INSIGHTS INTO THE LIFE OF JOSHUA

GENE GETZ

Fearless Leadership: Insights into the Life of Joshua
© 2004 Gene Getz

Published by Serendipity House Publishers
Nashville, Tennessee

ISBN: 1-5749-4144-5

Dewey Decimal Classification: 248.842
Subject Headings:
Joshua\Bible. O.T. Joshua--Study\Men--Religious Life

Unless otherwise indicated, all Scripture quotations are taken from the
Holman Christian Standard Bible®,
Copyright © 1999, 2000, 2002, 2003 by Holman Bible Publishers.
Used by permission.

To purchase additional copies of this resource or other studies:
ORDER ONLINE at www.SerendipityHouse.com;
VISIT the LifeWay Christian Store nearest you;
WRITE Serendipity House, 117 10th Avenue North, Nashville, TN 37234
FAX (615) 277-8181
PHONE (800) 525-9563

1-800-525-9563
www.SerendipityHouse.com

Printed in the United States of America
10 09 08 07 06 05 04   1 2 3 4 5 6 7 8 9 10

CONTENTS

FEARLESS LEADERSHIP

FEARLESS LEADERSHIP

A STUDY OF THE LIFE OF JOSHUA

Our battlefield is very different from the one Joshua fought on, but *faith is still the ultimate weapon!* Joshua was a dynamic leader, yet he literally trembled when God called him to succeed Moses. At times he was fearful, weak, or prone to bad judgments. Despite his humanness, an open heart, teachable spirit, humility, and faith, enabled him to learn from God how to be a great leader, fearlessly facing many of the same challenges we struggle with today. Whether leading in our homes, businesses, churches, or communities, God is calling us to step up, grasp His hand, and learn to lead a victorious Christian life.

The Men of Purpose series focuses on the lives of men in the Bible who provide poignant examples of godly masculinity. Each of these leaders faced trials, frustration, and failure, yet was inspired by God to achieve great goals. In a world where Christian male role models seem increasingly rare, this series reminds us that some of the most worthy examples of godly character can be found in the biblical figures who brought power, wisdom, and inspiration to God's people throughout the ages.

As you and your group approach each study, do so with the same spiritual passion and personal integrity that have characterized Dr. Getz throughout his lifetime. Let the goals of every group meeting be to understand biblical truths, to grapple with Dr. Getz' principles to live by, and to commit to helping each other apply what you learn in your daily lives. This is the supreme act of a disciple—being doers of God's Word (James 1:22-25).

HOW TO USE THIS BOOK

While this Bible study may be used individually, it is designed to be used within the context of small groups. Each group meeting should include all elements of the following "three-part agenda."

Icebreaker: Fun, history-giving questions are designed to warm up the group and build understanding between group members. You may choose to use all of the Icebreaker questions, especially if there is a new group member that will need help in feeling comfortable with the group.

One of the purposes of this book is to begin and to then solidify a group. Therefore, getting to know one another and bonding together are essential to the success of this effort. The Icebreaker segment in each group session is designed to help you become better acquainted, greatly enhancing your group experience.

Bible Study: The heart of each meeting is your examination together of the Bible. The questions are open discovery questions that lead to further inquiry. Reference notes are provided to give everyone a "level playing field" and provide deeper insights into the biblical story. This section emphasizes understanding what the Bible says and applying its truth to real life. The questions for each session build on one another. There are always "going deeper" questions provided. You should always leave time for the last of the "questions for interaction." You may elect to use the optional "going deeper" questions to lead you in applying what the group has learned. This segment also satisfies the desire for more challenging questions in groups that have been together for a while.

To help your men connect as a group, it is important for everyone to participate in the Bible study. There are no right or wrong answers to the questions. Participants should strive to make all of the other group members feel comfortable during the Bible Study time. Because we all have differing levels of biblical knowledge, it is essential that we understand and appreciate the personal context from which each one of us responds. We don't have to know much about theology and history to bring our own perspectives to bear on the truths contained in the Scriptures. It is vital to keep encouraging all group members to share what they are observing as you work through these important Bible passages.

Caring Time: All study should lead us to action. Each session ends with prayer and direction in caring for the needs of individual group members. You can choose between the various questions provided, or use them all.

Small groups help the larger body of Christ in many ways: caring for individuals, holding one another up in prayer, providing emotional support, and bringing new men into the church family. Each week it is important to remember to pray for those whom God would bring to your group.

HOW TO GET THE MOST OUT OF THIS BOOK

Begin by reviewing the following ground rules and talk about the importance of "sharing your story" (see below).

GROUND RULES

• **Priority**: While you are in the group, give the group meeting priority.

• **Participation**: Everyone participates and no one dominates.

• **Respect**: Everyone is given the right to their own opinion and all questions are encouraged ... and respected.

• **Confidentiality**: Anything that is said in the meeting is never repeated outside the meeting.

• **Empty Chair**: The group stays open to inviting new men to every meeting. The empty chair in your circle symbolizes those men you need to invite.

• **Support**: Permission is given to call upon each other in time of need—even in the middle of the night.

• **Advice Giving**: Unsolicited advice is not allowed.

• **Mission**: We agree to do everything in our power to work toward starting a new group—a vital part of our mission.

SHARING YOUR STORY

These sessions are designed to assist group members to share a little of their personal lives each time the group meets. Through a number of special techniques, each member is encouraged to move from low risk, less personal sharing to higher risk responses. This helps develop authentic community and facilitates care giving within your group.

It is only when group members begin to share their own stories that the group bonds at levels deep enough for life-change to take place.

PERSONAL NOTES

Basic Training for Life

Welcome

Perhaps more than any other Old Testament man, Joshua exemplifies for each of us how to live a victorious Christian life. He walked through the battlefields of the Old Testament as a godly man. Though he certainly made mistakes, he lived an exemplary life. God developed courageous leadership in his life that enabled him to fight and conquer daunting enemy armies.

What can a 21st century man living in a vastly different culture learn from a man like Joshua? His life demonstrates how men in any age can become courageous leaders "strengthened by the Lord and by His vast strength." You, like Joshua, can "put on the full armor of God" in order to defeat "the world powers of this darkness" and "the spiritual forces of evil in the heavens" (Eph. 6:10-12).

Icebreaker

Maturing is a lifelong adventure. It takes time. One of the fundamental lessons we need to learn is how to faithfully handle present responsibilities. Success at one level prepares us for success at the next level.

What a hard lesson to learn! We start life focused on ourselves and on having fun right here, right now. The transition to living this day in light of the unfolding drama of our entire lifetime is a major task of adulthood. *How are you doing?*

1. When you were a boy, if you wanted to learn to operate a yo-yo or some new electronic gadget, how did you go about it?
   a. Studied and practiced on my own until I had it perfect
   b. Worked at it hard for a few days and gave up
   c. Took a class or read a how-to book
   d. Hung out with my friends and picked up whatever they knew
   e. Was content to play at a basic level
   f. Other _____

2. What have been some key periods of time or key experiences that God has used to provide you the "basic training" required for your present adult life?

3. Who are some of the people God has used to provide your "basic training," shaping the way you handle adulthood?

BIBLICAL FOUNDATION

Joshua was born in Egypt, when the "new king, who had not known Joseph, came to power" (Ex. 1:8). Life was not easy in his early years. His father and mother were slaves along with all the children of Israel who were victimized by this Pharaoh. When Joshua grew older, he too became a "working" slave.

Joshua evidently was the firstborn son of his family (1 Chron. 7:27). He would remember all his life the horrific night and subsequent morning of the Passover (Ex. 12–13). By then he may already have started serving Moses, for we read that Joshua, the son of Nun, was an "assistant to Moses since his youth" (Num. 11:28).

Joshua served a long period of apprenticeship during which Moses developed unusual confidence in his young lieutenant. This is demonstrated in three unique experiences Joshua was given during the 40 years that he walked alongside Moses in the wasteland between Egypt and the promised land in Canaan.

Lessons from the Frontline

[8] At Rephidim, Amalek came and fought against Israel. [9] Moses said to Joshua, "Select some men for us, and go fight against Amalek. Tomorrow I will stand on the hilltop with God's staff in my hand."

[10] Joshua did as Moses had told him, and fought against Amalek, while Moses, Aaron, and Hur went up to the top of the hill. [11] While Moses held up his hand, Israel prevailed, but whenever he put his hand down, Amalek prevailed. [12] When Moses' hands grew heavy, they took a stone and put [it] under him, and he sat down on it. Then Aaron and Hur supported his hands, one on one side and one on the other so that his hands remained steady until the sun went down. [13] So Joshua defeated Amalek and his army with the sword.

[14] The Lord then said to Moses, "Write this down on a scroll as a reminder and recite it to Joshua: I will completely blot out the memory of Amalek under heaven."

Exodus 17:8-14

Lessons from Mount Sinai

¹² The Lord said to Moses, "Come up to Me on the mountain and stay there so that I may give you the stone tablets with the law and commands I have written for their instruction."

¹³ So Moses arose with his assistant Joshua, and went up the mountain of God. ¹⁴ He told the elders, "Wait here for us until we return to you. Aaron and Hur are here with you. Whoever has a dispute should go to them."

Exodus 24:12-14

⁷ Now Moses took a tent and set it up outside the camp, far away from the camp; he called it the tent of meeting. Anyone who wanted to consult the LORD would go to the tent of meeting that was outside the camp. ⁸ Whenever Moses went out to the tent, all the people would stand up, each one at the door of his tent, and they would watch Moses until he entered the tent. ⁹ When Moses entered the tent, the pillar of cloud would come down and remain at the entrance to the tent, and [the LORD] would speak with Moses. ¹⁰ As all the people saw the pillar of cloud remaining at the entrance to the tent, they would stand up, then bow in worship, each one at the door of his tent. ¹¹ The LORD spoke with Moses face to face, just as a man speaks with his friend. Then Moses would return to the camp, but his assistant, the young man Joshua son of Nun, would not leave the inside of the tent.

Exodus 33:7-11

Lessons from the Spy Mission

¹ The LORD spoke to Moses: ² Send men to scout out the land of Canaan I am giving to the Israelites. Send one man who is a leader among them from each of their ancestral tribes. ... ¹⁶ These were the names of the men Moses sent to scout out the land, and Moses renamed Hoshea son of Nun, Joshua.

¹⁷ When Moses sent them to scout out the land of Canaan, he told them, "Go up this way to the Negev, then go up into the hill country. ¹⁸ See what the land is like, and whether the people who live there are strong or weak, few or many. ¹⁹ Is the land they live in good or bad? Are the cities they live in encampments or fortifications? ²⁰ Is the land fertile or unproductive? Are there trees in it or not? Be courageous. Bring back some fruit from the land." ...

²⁶ The men went back to Moses, Aaron, and the entire Israelite community in the Wilderness of Paran at Kadesh. They brought back a report for them and the whole community, and they showed them the

fruit of the land. ... ³⁰ Then Caleb quieted the people in the presence of Moses and said, "We must go up and take possession of the land because we can certainly conquer it!"

³¹ But the men who had gone up with him responded, "We can't go up against the people because they are stronger than we are!" ³² So they gave a negative report to the Israelites about the land they had scouted: "The land we passed through to explore is one that devours its inhabitants, and all the people we saw in it are men of great size." ...

⁶ Joshua son of Nun and Caleb son of Jephunneh, who were among those who scouted out the land, tore their clothes ⁷ and said to the entire Israelite community: "The land we passed through and explored is an extremely good land. ⁸ If the LORD is pleased with us, He will bring us into this land, a land flowing with milk and honey, and give it to us." ... ¹⁰ While the whole community threatened to stone them, the glory of the LORD appeared to all the Israelites at the tent of meeting.

Numbers 13:1-2, 16-20a, 26, 30-32; 14:6-8, 10

PRINCIPLES TO LIVE BY

At some point, perhaps after the 12 spies returned from their mission in Canaan, Moses renamed his protégé. Originally his name had been Hoshea (Num. 13:8), but Moses began to call him Joshua (v. 16). Hoshea meant "salvation," while Joshua meant "the Lord is salvation." From a human point of view, Hoshea would save Israel, but from a divine point of view, *God* would lead Israel safely and victoriously into Canaan.

After a lengthy period of "basic training," Joshua clearly learned that God was the Savior of His people. Joshua's new name reflected the completion of his spiritual curriculum and continued to emphasize throughout his life this important truth that God alone was the source of power and salvation. He was now ready to allow God to use his abilities, skills, and all he had learned during his years of preparation.

PRINCIPLE 1

IT TAKES TIME TO PREPARE TO BE A FAITHFUL LEADER OF OTHERS.

Joshua's prominence in Israel came only after many years of dedicated service, both to the Lord and His commandments. Joshua faithfully served Moses, God's appointed leader, and proved himself worthy of trust.

Many men today want to bypass the process of demonstrating faithfulness over a period of time. In this sense, we're a product of our culture. We want instant recognition, instant prominence, and instant responsibility for fulfilling important leadership roles in God's great army, the Body of Christ. Furthermore, many of us already in leadership positions are too quick to appoint people to important spiritual responsibilities (see 1 Tim. 5:22).

PRINCIPLE 2

AS CHRISTIAN MEN, WE MUST REALIZE THE UNIQUE BALANCE BETWEEN DEPENDENCE ON GOD AND CONFIDENCE IN THE STRENGTHS AND ABILITIES THAT HE HAS CREATED IN US.

Without question God used the *man* Joshua to achieve His redemptive goals. But Joshua knew it was *God* Himself who would truly guide and direct Israel. It was His power that rolled back the waters of the Jordan (Josh. 3), His strength that caused the walls of Jericho to collapse (Josh. 6), and His wisdom that enabled Joshua to strategize against the enemies of Israel time and again.

This is a divine mystery. God *does* use our faithfulness, our commitment, and our human capacities and capabilities. But in reality, without Him, we'll accomplish little, and what we do achieve may turn out to be "wood, hay, or straw" with no lasting results (1 Cor. 3:12).

PRINCIPLE 3

WE MUST BEGIN TO SERVE GOD NOW IN ORDER TO PREPARE FOR FUTURE RESPONSIBILITY.

It takes time and preparation to equip us to handle important spiritual responsibilities. Spend time faithfully serving God in less demanding roles and learning from more mature and experienced men. In this sense, we all need mentors. Joshua's strength was deeply rooted in the lessons he learned from Moses. Just as Moses was his example, role model, and spiritual shepherd, we can all gain strength from a godly mentor.

Note also that Joshua served faithfully without even knowing that someday he would take over Moses' leadership role. This highlights another reason why God chose him and used him. Not only did he learn his lessons well, but his motives were pure.

QUESTIONS FOR INTERACTION

1. When you hear that Joshua spent 40 years in basic training as he
   prepared to succeed Moses, what is your first reaction? (Circle the best
   answer.)
   a. I could never wait that long. I want to lead now.
   b. Maybe there's hope for me out there someday.
   c. Patient faithfulness pays off.
   d. I have no interest in filling shoes that big.
   e. Other _____.

2. How do you feel about the idea of being mentored by a more seasoned
   leader in preparation for the future? (Again, circle your answer.)
   a. I learn better without someone looking over my shoulder.
   b. I would like to be able to consult with an experienced leader.
   c. I don't function well in groups.
   d. I'd like someone to give me regular feedback on my
      performance.
   e. I'd like to learn to lead through a discipling relationship.
   f. Other _____.

3. According to Exodus 17:8-14, what were Joshua's responsibilities in the
   battle against Amalek? Moses' responsibilities? God's responsibilities?

4. What early lessons about leadership do you think God wanted Joshua
   to learn from the encounter with Amalek?

5. What privileged access to the presence of the Lord did Joshua enjoy as
   Moses' assistant (Ex. 24:13; 33:11)?

6. What do you think God wanted Joshua to learn about leadership
   through observing Moses' relationship with Him?

7. What was the basic dispute between the Joshua/Caleb duo and the
   other 10 spies (Num. 13:26, 30-32; 14:6-8)?

8. What do you think God wanted Joshua to learn about leadership in
   Israel from the spying episode?

9. How did Joshua's training prepare him to have greater confidence both
   in God and in himself as God's man?

LESSON 1

13

GOING DEEPER

10. How does a man learn faithfulness in our modern world?

11. How can we balance both confidence in God *and* confidence in our training and God-given abilities?

12. What things has God given you to do now that might be training you for greater responsibility in the future? What makes you think so?

CARING TIME

In this group we are engaged in each other's "basic training" as we prepare for God's next assignments and future responsibilities. That's why we give the group high priority in our schedules, participate freely, respect one another's confidence, and support one another in every way we can.

1. What battles are you fighting in the world where you need someone to be lifting you up in prayer, just as Moses lifted his hands to God on Joshua' behalf (Ex. 17:11)?

2. How can we ensure that we share openly about the needs of our lives, and give one another support as we grow in Christ throughout this study on the life of Joshua?

3. Let's conclude by having each of us pray aloud one after the other for the man to our right, that he will benefit greatly from studying the life of Joshua.

NEXT WEEK

Next week we will find Joshua facing the daunting task of replacing the recently deceased Moses, Israel's deliverer and lawgiver. Joshua must have felt overwhelmed by the sheer magnitude of his new responsibility. God stepped in with a call to courage. Joshua already had absolute confidence in God's power and faithfulness. What he needed was the inner strength to step out in that faith. Too often we find it easier to verbalize our faith than to act on it. We too need to respond to God's call to be strong and courageous.

SCRIPTURE NOTES

EXODUS 17:8-14

17:8 Amalek. This was a nomadic tribe descended from Esau's grandson Amalek (Gen. 36:12, 16). Because Amalek attacked Israel without provocation as Israel traveled to Sinai, God decreed Amalek's destruction (Ex. 17:14).

17:9 Joshua. Moses chose a man who possessed military prowess. Both this incident and the conquest of Canaan 40 years later confirmed that Moses had picked the right man for the job. Joshua's faith in God made him a worthy leader of the Israelites (Deut. 34:9).

17:11 held up his hand. The soldiers fought the battle, but God determined the outcome. Moses held his staff above his head to appeal for God's help and to demonstrate Israel's total dependence on God for victory.

17:14 recite it to Joshua. During the invasion of Canaan, the Israelites under Joshua regarded Amalek as an enemy worthy of special attention because of God's message through Moses.

EXODUS 24:12-14; 33:7-11

24:12 instruction. The law and commands are not merely codes of conduct to be posted on a wall. They are divine commands to be taken seriously and to be studied and followed.

24:13 assistant. "Assistant" translates the Hebrew word for an elevated servant. Joshua was an invaluable aide to Moses in every area of his life and work. The Hebrew term does not have the idea of "slave," although Joseph, who was a slave, achieved the status of assistant or personal attendant in Potiphar's house (Gen. 39:4). Levites, first in the tabernacle and later the temple, wore this title as ministers or servants of God (Deut. 10:8; 1 Kings 8:11). In these passages, various English words appear to capture the elusive sense of this Hebrew noun.

33:7 tent. The tent mentioned here was different from the tabernacle. It was probably Moses' own tent which was a shrine, a place to pray and inquire of God. It sat outside of camp rather than in the center of it as did the tabernacle. The plans for the tabernacle were given to Moses starting in Exodus 25. The construction of the tabernacle is described starting in Exodus 35.
 33:8 the people would stand up. The people were looking to God in reverence. They stood off at a distance in awe of God.

33:9 the pillar of cloud. The presence of God was always visible in the Israelite camp during the 40-year journey from Egypt to Canaan. God displayed His presence as a pillar of cloud by day and a pillar of fire by night (Ex. 13:21). When the cloud or fire moved, the Israelites followed; when it stopped, they pitched camp (Num. 9:15-23).

33:11 as a man speaks with his friend. By this time, Moses had walked a long journey with God by his side. He had seen God in a burning bush, a cloud, and a pillar of fire. He had met with God on a mountain, in a desert, and in the middle of a miraculously dry seabed. He was a friend of God, an intimate friend. *Joshua.* Following Moses, Joshua was the soldier who led the people to conquer the promised land.

NUMBERS 13:1-2, 16-20A, 26, 30-32; 14:6-8, 10

13:2 from each of their ancestral tribes. This effort was organized much as was the census at the beginning of the book of Numbers. Selecting one from each tribe would give credibility and unity to their report. Caleb represented the tribe of Judah (v. 6) and Joshua represented the tribe of Ephraim (v. 8), historically the two dominant tribes of Israel.

13:17-20 strong or weak, few or many. Moses had very explicit instructions for the group of spies who were being sent to Canaan. The spies were not only to bring back a report of the land itself but also of the type of people who occupied the land.

13:30 Caleb. Only Caleb is mentioned here, but we know that Joshua also believed that they should trust God and enter the land of Canaan because 10 spies brought a negative report and there were 12 spies in all.

13:32 a negative report. The people had endured hardships (and not happily) to come to this place God had promised them, only to hear that the Canaanites could easily destroy them. Their sense of disappointment reflected a serious lack of faith. The word buzzing around camp was that God had brought them this far only to forsake them. From the time of Abraham, God had required that His people live by faith. But this cynical report rattled the people so they were doubtful and dismayed.

14:6 tore their clothes. Joshua and Caleb felt deep distress over the disobedience of their fellow Israelites and expressed their grief in the most vivid way they knew within their culture. Ripping their clothes captured the attention of the multitude and gave the two loyal spies a dramatic opportunity to speak on behalf of the promises of God.

14:10 glory of the LORD. God makes Himself known to all people. The Israelites were fuming and fussing, not about the leadership of Moses and Aaron, but against God Himself.

PERSONAL NOTES

SUPERNATURAL COURAGE & BLESSING

LAST WEEK

In the first lesson we saw how God prepared Joshua to succeed Moses as the leader of Israel. For 40 years Moses mentored his loyal assistant as Israel wandered in the wilderness. Joshua fought the enemies who attacked the camp (Ex. 17:8-14). He also scouted in Canaan as one of the 12 spies (Num. 13–14). He developed spiritually as he ascended Mount Sinai with Moses to receive the Ten Commandments (Ex. 24:13), and he guarded the tent of meeting where Moses sought guidance from the Lord (Ex. 33:11). During this time, Joshua became a military master who engineered the strategy that divided and conquered the promised land.

ICEBREAKER

Courage presupposes fear. Only when circumstances threaten us do we need a strong heart and a tenacious faith in God's care. Courage doesn't pretend dangers aren't real. That's foolhardiness. Courage is strength of heart and mind to face fearsome circumstances with the resources at hand which include our personal capabilities, the assistance of others, and most importantly, God and His Word.

1. What was your most frightening experience when you were a boy?
   When you were a child, who comforted you when you were afraid?

2. Who can you turn to today when you are fearful?

3. In what ways do you rely on God when you are afraid or anxious?

BIBLICAL FOUNDATION

Just before his death, Moses "laid his hands" on Joshua and commissioned him to lead the Israelite nation into Canaan. He performed this ceremony in the presence of all Israel (Deut. 34:9). Joshua was a brave man and well prepared. He had the confidence of Moses and, more importantly, of the Lord. Yet, when the time came to take the reins of leadership, Joshua was consumed by fear. He understood only too well the awesomeness of God's charge and what lay ahead.

Self-Confidence and God-Confidence

[1] After the death of Moses the Lord's servant, the Lord spoke to Joshua son of Nun, who had served Moses: [2] "Moses My servant is dead. Now you and all the people prepare to cross over the Jordan to the land I am giving the Israelites. [3] I have given you every place where the sole of your foot treads, just as I promised Moses. [4] Your territory will be from the wilderness and Lebanon to the great Euphrates River—all the land of the Hittites—and west to the Mediterranean Sea. [5] No one will be able to stand against you as long as you live. I will be with you, just as I was with Moses. I will not leave you or forsake you.

[6] "Be strong and courageous for you will distribute the land I swore to their fathers to give them as an inheritance. [7] Above all, be strong and very courageous to carefully observe the whole instruction My servant Moses commanded you. Do not turn from it to the right or the left, so that you will have success wherever you go. [8] This book of instruction must not depart from your mouth; you are to recite it day and night, so that you may carefully observe everything written in it. For then you will prosper and succeed in whatever you do. [9] Haven't I commanded you: be strong and courageous? Do not be afraid or discouraged, for the Lord your God is with you wherever you go."

[10] Then Joshua commanded the officers of the people: [11] "Go through the camp and tell the people, 'Get provisions ready for yourselves, for within three days you will be crossing the Jordan to go in and take possession of the land the Lord your God is giving you to inherit.' "

[12] Joshua said to the Reubenites, the Gadites, and half the tribe of Manasseh: [13] "Remember what Moses the Lord's servant commanded you when he said, 'The Lord your God will give you rest, and He will give you this land.' [14] Your wives, young children, and livestock may remain in the land Moses gave you on this side of the Jordan. But your fighting men must cross over in battle formation ahead of your brothers and help them [15] until the Lord gives our brothers rest, as [He has given] you, and they too possess the land the Lord your God is giving them. You may then return to the land of your inheritance and take possession of what Moses the Lord's servant gave you on the east side of the Jordan."

[16] They answered Joshua, "Everything you have commanded us we will do, and everywhere you send us we will go. [17] We will obey you, just as we obeyed Moses in everything. And may the Lord your God be with

you, as He was with Moses. [18] Anyone who rebels against your order and does not obey your words in all that you command him, will be put to death. Above all, be strong and courageous!"

Joshua 1:1-18

PRINCIPLES TO LIVE BY

Life is filled with threatening situations. To act responsibly and proactively calls for daily courage in our marriages, our families, our neighborhoods, and our churches. The business world in particular is highly competitive and filled will all sorts of challenges. One of these challenges is to live ethically when the people around us do not.

One of our greatest temptations as men is to allow our egos to control us to the point that we try to solve problems in our own strength . We've come a long way in our spiritual growth when we can accept that we truly do need God and others to succeed. Our culture of rugged individualism says, "Be a man—stand on your own two feet and go it alone." But in the Bible, courage is learned and expressed in relationship with God and others, not in isolation.

PRINCIPLE 1

LIKE JOSHUA, WE CAN AND MUST LEARN TO "BE STRONG AND COURAGEOUS," WHATEVER OUR RESPONSIBILITIES OR POSITION IN LIFE.

All of us have human weaknesses in the form of fears, anxieties, and feelings of inadequacy. God understood all of these problems in Joshua's life and reassured him and helped him to rise above his frustrating and threatening circumstances.

God also understands our humanness. He made us. He knows us. He sympathizes with us. There is no struggle with which He does not identify. He does not stand over us ready to condemn us in moments of weakness. Rather, He is reaching out to help and reassure us, just as He did for Joshua!

The Lord dealt with Joshua's fear by reminding him of His previous promises to Israel regarding the promised land, reassuring him of the certainty of His presence and promises. He charged his servant to become thoroughly familiar with His law, to apply it to his own life, and then to clearly and consistently communicate it to all the children of Israel. Just so, our strength and authority must be based on the utterly dependable Word of God.

In the first chapter of this dynamic historical book, the Lord shared with Joshua a very important secret for successful spiritual living and leadership: *obedience to His Word brings blessing*. Rest assured that this is an ongoing promise throughout Scripture and applicable to all believers. God always honors obedience to His Word.

With this principle in mind, Paul wrote, "Do not be conformed to this age, but be transformed by the renewing of your mind, so that you may discern what is the good, pleasing, and perfect will of God" (Rom. 12:2). The great news is that the blessings from God are not only for this life, but for all eternity. The most important blessing for obedience to God's Word will be His personal commendation and reward, "Well done, good and faithful servant; you were faithful over a few things, I will make you ruler over many things. Enter into the joy of your lord" (Matt 25:21, NKJV).

PRINCIPLE 3

GOD WILL NEVER LEAVE US OR FORSAKE US.

"Haven't I commanded you: be strong and courageous? Do not be afraid or discouraged, for the LORD your God is with you wherever you go" (Josh. 1:9). These must have been the most reassuring words that God spoke to Joshua. The Lord Himself promised to be his continual companion and divine, all-powerful resource.

Jeremiah shared this same promise in a moving and encouraging way, "Because of the Lord's faithful love we do not perish, for His mercies never end. They are new every morning; great is Your faithfulness!" (Lam. 3:22-23). And when Jesus charged the apostles with the Great Commission, He promised—"I am with you always, to the end of the age" (Matt. 28:20).

LESSON 2

1. Name two challenging areas in your life in which you wish God would personally show up and encourage you to be strong and courageous.

2. Which of the following best describes your typical level of courage?
   a. Brave heart
   b. Chicken heart
   c. Reluctant heart
   d. Anxious heart
   e. Other _____

3. Read Joshua 1:1-18 and underline or highlight every occurrence of the words "be strong and courageous." How many did you find? In each case, who is speaking this encouragement to Joshua?

4. In verses 1-6, for what task did Joshua need strength and courage?

5. In verses 7-9, for what other task did Joshua need strength and courage? How does this task relate to the first one in verses 1-6?

6. Joshua needed strength and courage for yet another task identified in verses 10-18. What was it and how was this challenge different? Why did Joshua need the affirmation of the people at this point?

7. Do you find it more frightening to formulate a major plan or to actually take the first concrete step to implement it? Which step do you imagine Joshua feared more?

8. Do you think prosperity and success are God's special reward for obeying His Word or the natural result of obeying His Word (Josh. 1:8)? Why?

9. Which of these best describes a step you could take to develop greater courage?
   a. Stop expecting to fail.
   b. Learn and obey God's Word.
   c. Expect God to help me.
   d. Dare to take risks.
   e. Depend more on others. Stop going it alone.
   f. Other _____.

LESSON 2

Going Deeper

10. In what areas of your life do you need to exercise more courage? Why?

11. What deficiencies in knowing or obeying God's Word do you need to address in order to "prosper and succeed" (Josh. 1:8)?

12. List ways you remind yourself when you're afraid or worried that God will never forsake you? How can you encourage others?

Caring Time

It takes courage to be a loving husband, caring father, hardworking employee, or loyal friend. Unfortunately, we have opportunities every day to live selfishly in our homes, dishonestly on our jobs, and carelessly in our friendships. When we face temptations, it takes daily commitment and courage to live by God's Word. However, it's along the rugged path of commitment and courage that we learn real success.

There will always be life challenges that frighten us. Do we really believe that God cares about *us* and *our* situations as much as He did about Joshua as the leader of Israel? He does. He says to each of us, "Haven't I commanded you: be strong and courageous? Do not be afraid or discouraged, for the LORD your God is with you wherever you go" (Josh. 1:9).

1. What is your greatest need for courage or assurance right now? Ask the men in our group to stand with you in prayer this week.

2. Do you have enough courage to share a step you'd like to take this week to begin improving your obedience to God's Word?

3. Who are some men we can invite to fill our "empty seat"? Who would benefit from studying courageous leadership?

Next Week

Next week we will meet Rahab, one of those fantastically unlikely people of faith we find in the Bible. Her line of work was repulsive. She had little or no theological training to prepare her to believe in the living God. Yet somehow her heart opened to rumors of the God of Israel, and she risked her life for Him and the spies who hid in her house. Her vigorous, active faith will challenge you to trust God more.

LESSON 2

JOSHUA 1:1-18

1:1-18 In an encounter resembling a scene from a presidential inauguration, God charged Joshua with his duties as he stood before the people he would lead. He would not forget God's repetitious challenge to be strong and courageous as he led the people of Israel into their promised land. Now, with the whole nation summoned together, the people affirmed God's choice for their leader and eagerly looked forward to God's blessings that they would receive under Joshua's command.

1:1 Joshua ...who had served Moses. Although he did not campaign for this position as Moses' assistant, Joshua consistently rose through the ranks. He served as captain of Moses' army, as well as one of the more exuberant and experienced spies sent into the land of Canaan (Ex. 17:9-14; 33:11; Deut. 31:23).

1:4 Your territory. This promised land was a long time in coming. Generations earlier, God promised it to Abraham (Gen. 13:14-17). Nearly 40 years earlier as a middle-aged man, Joshua had spied out the land (Num. 13:16). Now in his 80s, Joshua would finally lead his people to conquer most of Canaan.

1:5 I will not leave you. Although Joshua was God's chosen leader, he likely experienced some fears at this defining moment. Despite any fears, power came as a result of God's presence, and this presence guaranteed the promises of blessing and success.

1:7 that you will have success. In today's world, success is most often a result of hard work and self-motivation. But God offered success as a gift of love to His people.

1:10 Joshua commanded. Imagine Joshua's voice snapping instructions to his officers. The inauguration was over. It was time for this new leader to take charge and lead his people on.

1:11 giving you to inherit. To these wandering fugitives, having a land of their own must have seemed like a dream. Joshua's leadership was forthright and inspiring for a people who needed a home and a vision.

1:12-15 possess the land. Although some of the Israelites were already unpacked and settled in parts of the newly conquered land, it would take the entire army to finish the conquest across the Jordan.

1:14 ahead of your brothers. As a symbol of unity, the fighting men who were already settled in the previously conquered land would march ahead of the others. Strong and courageous, they would lead by example.

1:18 will be put to death. Success was the only option for the resolute Israelites. Any distractions from their goal had to be eliminated. Any rebellion in their ranks would not be tolerated.

PERSONAL NOTES

GOD'S TRANSFORMING POWER

LAST WEEK

In the second lesson of this study we saw how God repeatedly encouraged Joshua for the big job of replacing Moses as the leader of Israel. Joshua wasn't a timid man, given to cowardice and self-doubt. He was a forceful leader used to being followed and obeyed. Yet, no matter what our temperament, whether we are filled with confidence or filled with fears, God wants us to know that He will be with us in every endeavor He sends us on. He wants us to learn, just as Joshua did, that our prosperity and success stem from confidence in God and obedience to His Word.

ICEBREAKER

A shared faith in Jesus as Savior brings together people who might otherwise never associate with one another. God is no respecter of persons. When He builds His Son's church, He seems to take great pleasure in populating it with the widest possible assortment of people.

1. How would you characterize the membership of this group of men?
    a. As alike as peas in a pod
    b. A butcher, a baker, and a candlestick maker
    c. Like comparing apples and frogs
    d. Cats and dogs loving the same master
    e. Other _____

2. Who's the most unusual person God has ever used to strengthen your life as a Christian? What contribution did this person make?

3. When have you seen a church embrace a person that polite society might consider "disreputable"? What was the result of that acceptance?

BIBLICAL FOUNDATION

When Joshua prepared to invade Canaan, he sent only two spies to scope out the land. Twelve spies had proven a cumbersome and divisive intelligence party 40 years before (Num. 13). Joshua sent the spies out for military reasons, but God also had a providential purpose for them. He intended to rescue a prostitute who had recently come to believe in Him, along with her entire family.

The Canaanites must have had the Israelite camp under surveillance because the number and movement of the spies were immediately known. The king of Jericho received word as soon as the spies entered Rahab's house, and he assumed that he had them cornered.

Weak in Theology; Dynamic in Faith

[1] Joshua son of Nun secretly sent two men as spies from Acacia Grove, saying, "Go and scout the land, especially Jericho." So they left, and they came to the house of a woman, a prostitute named Rahab, and stayed there.

[2] The king of Jericho was told, "Look, some of the Israelite men have come here tonight to investigate the land." [3] Then the king of Jericho sent [word] to Rahab and said, "Bring out the men who came to you and entered your house, for they came to investigate the entire land."

[4] But the woman had taken the two men and hidden them. So she said, "Yes, the men did come to me, but I didn't know where they were from. [5] At nightfall, when the gate was about to close, the men went out, and I don't know where they were going. Chase after them quickly, and you can catch up with them!" [6] But she had taken them up to the roof and hidden them among the stalks of flax that she had arranged on the roof. [7] The men pursued them along the road to the fords of the Jordan, and as soon as they left to pursue them, the gate was shut.

[8] Before the men fell asleep, she went up on the roof [9] and said to them, "I know that the Lord has given you this land and that dread of you has fallen on us, and everyone who lives in the land is panicking because of you. [10] For we have heard how the Lord dried up the waters of the Red Sea before you when you came out of Egypt, and what you did to Sihon and Og, the two Amorite kings you completely destroyed across the Jordan. [11] When we heard this, we lost heart, and everyone's courage failed because of you, for the Lord your God is God in heaven above and on earth below. [12] Now please swear to me by the Lord that you will also show kindness to my family, because I showed kindness to you. Give me a sure sign [13] that you will spare the lives of my father, mother, brothers, sisters, and all who belong to them, and save us from death."

[14] The men answered her, "[We will give] our lives for yours. If you don't report our mission, we will show kindness and faithfulness to you

when the Lord gives us the land."

¹⁵ Then she let them down by a rope through the window, since she lived in a house that was [built] into the wall of the city. ¹⁶ "Go to the hill country so that the men pursuing you won't find you," she said to them. "Hide yourselves there for three days until they return; afterwards, go on your way."

¹⁷ The men said to her, "We will be free from this oath you made us swear, ¹⁸ unless, when we enter the land, you tie this scarlet cord to the window through which you let us down. Bring your father, mother, brothers, and all your father's family into your house. ¹⁹ If anyone goes out the doors of your house, his blood will be on his own head, and we will be innocent. But if anyone with you in the house should be harmed, his blood will be on our heads. ²⁰ And if you report our mission, we are free from the oath you made us swear."

²¹ "Let it be as you say," she replied, and she sent them away. After they had gone, she tied the scarlet cord to the window.

²² So the two men went into the hill country and stayed there three days until the pursuers had returned. They searched all along the way, but did not find them. ²³ Then the men returned, came down from the hill country, and crossed [the Jordan]. They went to Joshua son of Nun and reported everything that had happened to them. ²⁴ They told Joshua, "The Lord has handed over the entire land to us. Everyone who lives in the land is also panicking because of us."

Joshua 2:1-24

PRINCIPLES TO LIVE BY

Rahab was spiritually ahead of many of the children of Israel, even though their light was greater. They had seen miracle after miracle, whereas Rahab had only heard about them. The children of Israel had received God's law by His direct revelation to Moses, whereas Rahab only heard indirectly about God's will. In the midst of an idolatrous and sinful city, Rahab came to know and serve the true and living God, even to the point of risking her own life. God gave greater attention to Rahab's faith because she was more faithful to the light that she had. The Lord honored her faith by including her in the Old Testament hall of fame (Heb. 11:31).

Rahab probably changed her spiritual allegiance some months before the spies arrived. The quantity of flax on her roof suggests that she had previously abandoned prostitution to become a cloth maker. The ancients had found a way to saturate ropes with concentrated dye. They would then cut a small length from the rope to soak in a vat to color a batch of cloth. Possession of a long rope like the one Rahab used to assist the spies, suggests large-scale cloth manufacturing. Rahab had changed careers as she responded in simple faith to the God whose grace extends to the darkest corners of the earth.

PRINCIPLE 1

GOD IS NO RESPECTER OF PERSONS.

The greatest lesson that jumps off the pages of Joshua chapter 2 is that God is no respecter of persons. Why else would He give so much space in the midst of divine history to record the conversion of Rahab? God's desire is that all people know that Jesus Christ died for the sins of the world. There's not a single individual outside the sphere of His love and grace (John 3:16-17).

There's another intriguing fact from this story that demonstrates God's love for sinners. Since Rahab had become a believer, why then would God choose to record her name in the New Testament as "Rahab the prostitute" (Heb. 11:31)? Why didn't He simply identify her as "Rahab the believer"? Was it not to demonstrate that He indeed is no respecter of persons and that all men and women everywhere can call on the name of the Lord and be saved (Rom. 10:13)?

Rahab entered Israel with a name of shame. And yet, she was, a woman of faith, redeemed and honored by the Lord of heaven. When Rahab believed God, He credited her faith to her as righteousness, just as He had done for Abraham (Rom. 4:22). Rahab's true legacy was not her prostitution, but her radical transformation and participation in God's plan of redemption. Amazingly, her name appears in the genealogy of Jesus Christ, the Savior of the world (Matt. 1:5).

PRINCIPLE 2

TRUE FAITH PRODUCES WORKS.

Faith is an action word. James wrote, "Faith, if it doesn't have works, is dead by itself" (Jas. 2:17). Rahab had a faith that propelled her into action. In that sense, she was "justified by works" (Jas. 2:25). She was saved by faith (Rom. 5:1) but proved her faith was real by her works of obedience and self-sacrifice.

The quality of Rahab's faith stands out in at least four ways.

First, she took God at His word. Rahab's first words to the spies were "I know" (Josh. 2:9). She believed that the God of Israel was the one true God and that He alone could be trusted.

Second, Rahab took a stand. Her faith produced self-denial. In protecting God's messengers, she denied everything her countrymen stood for. She was no longer a part of sin-filled Jericho. Her life and allegiance changed, and people noticed it.

Third, Rahab's faith caused her to show concern for others. She cared for the spies and helped them escape. She convinced her family to come to her house and stay there seven days as the army of Israel encircled Jericho. She did not know when the fatal blow would fall, but she persevered in her concern.

Fourth, she simply believed God. Rahab's theology was simple, but her faith was great. She knew very little about God and His covenant with His people, but she acted strongly on what little she did know.

QUESTIONS FOR INTERACTION

1. Which of these descriptions best reflects the relationship between your theological knowledge and your faith in action?
   a. Little theology; lots of faith
   b. Lots of theology; little faith
   c. Little theology; little faith
   d. Lots of theology; lots of faith
   e. Other _____

2. Who do you identify with most in the Rahab story and why?
   a. The spies
   b. Rahab
   c. The king's searchers
   d. Joshua
   e. Rahab's family

3. How did the king of Jericho appeal to Rahab's patriotism in his search for the spies (Josh. 2:2-3)?

4. What did Rahab hope to gain by protecting the spies (vv. 12-13)?

5. What agreement did the spies make with Rahab (vv. 14, 17-20)?

6. How did Rahab keep the soldiers of Jericho and the Israelite spies from stumbling onto one another outside the city (vv. 5-7, 15-16, 22-23)?

7. What did the spies report to Joshua (vv. 23-24)?

8. Which of these do you think best explains why Rahab did what she did? Why?
   a. She played both sides: if Jericho won, she stayed put; if Israel won, she joined them.
   b. She believed Israel would win and changed sides to save her neck.
   c. She was superstitious and therefore afraid of the strange God of Israel.
   d. She believed the Lord alone "is God in heaven above and on earth below" and had a true spiritual conversion.
   e. Other _____.

9. In spite of her reputation and her obvious lie, why does the New Testament regard Rahab as an example of sterling faith (Heb. 11:31; Jas. 2:25)?

GOING DEEPER

10. Given the amount of biblical and theological knowledge you have, how strong do you think your active faith *should* be?

11. Why does God take such great pleasure in accepting the often shaky faith of people with a wretched past?

12. How do you think the church could do better in accepting and encouraging seekers with shameful reputations and immoral backgrounds?

CARING TIME

Rahab and the two spies huddled together on her rooftop formed a small group of sorts. They had to speak openly and truthfully. They made a covenant to take care of one another. God's plans for their lives formed the basis of all they did together. They all acted on the basis of those plans. Their lives were changed forever because they had been together.

Our group needs the same dynamic theirs had. We need to accept one another unconditionally, no matter what our backgrounds. As the church, we should be free to share our deepest fears, darkest sins, and brightest dreams in order to go forward together in an environment of safety and support. Finally, we need to act boldly on every scrap of faith in God that we possess.

1. How might our group unintentionally make other guys feel they aren't good enough to join us?

2. How can we become less superficial and more transparent in how we share our lives and concerns with one another?

3. How can we pray for you that you would act out your faith more boldly?

NEXT WEEK

Next week we will see Joshua lead Israel across the Jordan River. Even though Israel was moving into territory bristling with hostile armies and fortifications, the river crossing was more of a spiritual exercise than a military one. Over the next three lessons it will become evident that God was much more concerned about the spirits of His people than about their weapons. Maybe we should change the old saying from "An army marches on its stomachs" to "An army marches on its hearts."

SCRIPTURE NOTES

JOSHUA 2:1-24

2:1-24 The theme of this story is risk. Rahab, the prostitute, risked her own life by harboring Joshua's spies. The spies themselves took great risk by trusting Rahab's instructions and her vow of silence. As a result of their combined risk, Joshua received the go-ahead from the spies' report and prepared to conquer the city of Jericho.

2:1 Acacia Grove. This translates the Hebrew name *Abel-shittim*, and probably identifies the most striking physical feature of the town. Acacia wood is hard-grained and repels insects. The ark of the covenant and the wooden portions of the tabernacle were made of acacia wood (Ex. 36:20; 37:1). *came to the house of . . . a prostitute.* City prostitutes in the ancient world often ran inns. This simplified procurement of clients. The spies, on their part, were seeking no more than lodging in a public house where information could be overheard.

2:2 the king of Jericho. Many cities of the ancient Near East were independent city-states with hereditary monarchs. See the list of city-state kings in Genesis 14:1-2 and Joshua 12:9-24.

2:4 So she said. Rahab lied to the king's men. There are three primary views about lying to protect someone. (1) In extreme circumstances, a lie is acceptable behavior. (2) A lie is always wrong, but sometimes it is a lesser wrong than the consequences of telling the truth. (3) A lie is always wrong. An alternative to lying must be found. In Rahab's case, it's hard to imagine avoiding a lie without giving away the spies. Yet, we must avoid the temptation to let the ends justify the means.

2:6 she had taken them up. The flax she was drying on her flat roof made a perfect hiding spot for her fugitives. **stalks of flax.** Flax is the source of the fibers from which linen is made. Flax stalks were soaked in water to separate the fibers from the stem. The fibers were pulled apart and spread on flat rooftops to dry in the sun before being woven into linen.

2:8-11 the LORD your God is God. No one ever taught Rahab as a child not to talk to strangers. In fact, she put a strange amount of faith in two people she hardly knew. And why was she so convinced of their God? After all, she was a prostitute, not a parishioner. Even so, Rahab heard about the wonders the Lord performed for Israel and believed in Him. Her fellow countrymen quaked in dread, but they did not turn to God in faith. Consequently Rahab is honored in the New Testament as a woman of great faith (Heb. 11:31) and became a part of Jesus' lineage (Matt. 1:5).

2:12 Give me a sure sign. Realizing she had spared their lives, Rahab took the opportunity to negotiate a tremendous favor from the two spies. Perhaps strengthened by her own confession, she wanted their assurance that the physical and also spiritual health of her family would be protected.

2:14 our lives for yours. A serious transaction had taken place and bonded three total strangers. Rahab rescued them from certain death. Rahab herself would soon barely escape the destruction of her city.

2:15 [built] into the wall of the city. Rahab likely made her home – an original high-rise apartment – on planks supported between the two walls surrounding the city of Jericho.

2:16 the hill country. Rahab sent the spies deeper into Canaan. Jericho lay below sea level in the Jordan Valley. The hills west of Jericho soared more than 3,000 feet above sea level and offered countless hiding places within their rugged heights. The king's soldiers meanwhile had hurried east to guard the fords of the Jordan (v. 7).

2:18 scarlet cord. To distinguish Rahab's house from the dozens of other houses in Jericho, the Israelites would look for a dyed cord dangling from her window. Rahab eagerly hung the cord, a symbol of her faith, as soon as the men left. The scarlet color of the cord hung upon her window as a symbol of her salvation and a sign that all in her house were to be protected is reminiscent of the Passover in Egypt (Ex. 11-12) and another preview of Jesus' blood shed for our salvation.

2:19 his blood will be on his own head. The spies took responsibility for the chance of a mistake. If anyone in Rahab's family were harmed during the attack, the spies would take the blame. However, if a member of the family left the safety of Rahab's house, the Israelites could not be held responsible.

2:22 into the hill country . . . three days. Hiding spots by the dozens awaited the spies as they traveled toward this cave-ridden area of Palestine. Since they were reported to have left through the city gate, the king's men looked for them along the road to the Jordan River.

A MIRACLE OF FAITH

LAST WEEK

Last week we interacted around the story of the two Israelite spies
and Rahab the prostitute. We saw how Rahab, on the basis of very little
theological information about the God of Israel, believed, trusted, and
did great works of faith. On the basis of her faithfulness we learned that
God is no respecter of persons and that real faith always results in works of
righteousness.

ICEBREAKER

God shows His power to different people in different ways. Some
see Him in the beauty of nature. Some discover Him in works of art.
Others discover God as the last resort during tragedies. A few find Him in
inexplicable events that seem to be miracles. Even in a group no larger than
ours, we have almost certainly experienced God in many different ways.

1. What's the earliest experience of God you can remember?
    a. Bible stories and prayer at home
    b. Sunday school or church
    c. The witness of a friend
    d. The faith of a girlfriend or wife
    e. A dream or vision
    f. The death of a family member or friend
    g. Other _____

2. Why did your family come to the town where you grew up? What's
   your favorite story about that move, whenever it occurred?

3. When have you witnessed an event that may have been a miracle? How
   did you react to it?

BIBLICAL FOUNDATION

When Joshua's two spies returned from Jericho, they were enthusiastic
about entering the land of Canaan. Their eager report contrasted sharply
with the disheartening report of the 10 spies who had scouted Canaan 40

years before (Num. 13:26-33). God used the positive reinforcement of the spies' good news to bolster Joshua's faith for the great challenge that lay immediately ahead.

Getting Their Feet Wet

[1] Joshua started early the next morning and left Acacia Grove with all the Israelites. They went as far as the Jordan and stayed there before crossing. [2] After three days the officers went through the camp [3] and commanded the people: "When you see the ark of the covenant of the Lord your God carried by the Levitical priests, you must break camp and follow it. [4] But keep a distance of about 1,000 yards between yourselves and the ark. Don't go near it, so that you can see the way to go, for you haven't traveled this way before."

[5] Joshua told the people, "Consecrate yourselves, because the Lord will do wonders among you tomorrow." [6] Then he said to the priests, "Take the ark of the covenant and go on ahead of the people." So they carried the ark of the covenant and went ahead of them.

[7] The Lord spoke to Joshua: "Today I will begin to exalt you in the sight of all Israel, so they will know that I will be with you just as I was with Moses. [8] Command the priests carrying the ark of the covenant: 'When you reach the edge of the waters, stand in the Jordan.' "

[9] Then Joshua told the Israelites, "Come closer and listen to the words of the Lord your God." [10] He said, "You will know that the living God is among you and that He will certainly dispossess before you the Canaanites, Hittites, Hivites, Perizzites, Girgashites, Amorites, and Jebusites [11] when the ark of the covenant of the Lord of all the earth goes ahead of you into the Jordan. [12] Now choose 12 men from the tribes of Israel, one man for each tribe. [13] When the feet of the priests who carry the ark of the Lord, the Lord of all the earth, come to rest in the Jordan's waters, its waters will be cut off. The water flowing downstream will stand up [in] a mass."

[14] When the people broke camp to cross the Jordan, the priests carried the ark of the covenant ahead of the people. [15] Now the Jordan overflows its banks throughout the harvest season. But as soon as the priests carrying the ark reached the Jordan, their feet touched the water at its edge [16] and the water flowing downstream stood still, rising up [in] a mass that extended as far as Adam, a city next to Zarethan. The water flowing downstream into the Sea of the Arabah (the Dead Sea) was completely cut off, and the people crossed opposite Jericho. [17] The priests carrying the ark of the Lord's covenant stood firmly on

dry ground in the middle of the Jordan, while all Israel crossed on dry ground until the entire nation had finished crossing the Jordan.

Joshua 3:1-17

PRINCIPLES TO LIVE BY

In the Bible, God doesn't usually speak to large groups of people. He speaks to one person or a few individuals, and they function as God's mouthpieces to relay His message to the target audience of believers or unbelievers. At the time of the invasion of Canaan, God spoke to and through Joshua.

There is much for us to learn from how Joshua received and responded to God's message, as well as how he handled the challenges of obeying it and passing it on. Even though Joshua was struggling with feelings of insecurity at the prospect of replacing Moses, he responded with great maturity and humility during this first major test of leadership.

PRINCIPLE 1

GOD HONORS FAITH, BUT HE DOES NOT EXPECT HIS CHILDREN TO OPERATE ON BLIND FAITH.

Joshua's work of faith was not based on some inner thoughts or intuitive feelings. It was based on facts. God spoke, not through some inner voice or existential experience, but through direct revelation. When God said to Joshua, "I will be with you just as I was with Moses" (Josh. 3:7), Joshua understood clearly the meaning of that promise. He also understood the significance of God's specific instructions to the priests about walking into the waters of the Jordan carrying the ark (v. 6).

Today many Christians are being led astray by relying totally on experience and feelings, which are in some instances in direct opposition to the written Word of God. Experience, even that which may appear to be *Christian* experience, can lead us into some very subtle traps. We must always make sure our feelings and desires (and faith) are in harmony with Scripture.

PRINCIPLE 2

GOD HONORS CHRISTIANS WHO PUT HIM FIRST.

God used Joshua's talents, gifts, and abilities. He had proven himself many times. He was a brilliant strategist. But, when it came to telling the children of Israel about God's plan, he completely bypassed the opportunity to exalt himself. God had said to him, "Today I will begin to exalt you in the sight of all Israel" (Josh. 3:7). Joshua in turn conveyed to the people, "You will know that the living God is among you" (v. 10).

This does not mean that we should not accept honor and praise, but rather it means that we should develop the ability to handle them with balance and perspective. The more we become secure within ourselves and in our position in Christ, the more we will be able to praise and honor God and others with naturalness and balance.

Often people with a self-image problem react to success like a dry sponge responds to water. They overreact with displays of pride or false humility. Your own temptation toward pride may be accentuated by feelings of insecurity and a lack of self-worth. If this is so, you need to refocus on who you are as a child of God and develop a proper sense of your exalted identity in Christ alone. Then you will be better able to give God His proper honor.

PRINCIPLE 3

GOD IS STILL REACHING OUT TO LOST PEOPLE.

The miracle that stopped the flow of the Jordan River for several hours was heard and seen for miles around. Every king and every commoner on both sides of the Jordan River had to be aware of what God had done. In addition to exalting Joshua in the eyes of Israel, the miracle declared the power and majesty of the God of Israel to the surrounding pagan nations.

Every Canaanite man, woman, and child could have turned to God in faith, as Rahab did, and been saved. By broadcasting His presence and His might, the Lord gave the inhabitants of Canaan another opportunity to turn from their gods of wood, stone, and metal. He is patient, "not wanting any to perish, but all to come to repentance" (2 Pet. 3:9). God wanted to use Israel in the Old Testament era as His communicators of righteousness and love to the surrounding world. Today He desires to use the church, the body of Christ, to proclaim this truth to those who do not know Him. We must never regard God's actions and blessings as divine gifts that stop with us. We are blessed to be a blessing. Whenever we do not pass on to others what we have received, we short-circuit God's outreach to a lost world.

Questions for Interaction

1. What challenge are you currently facing where you need clear direction from God?

2. Where are you most likely to receive God's direction about the challenge you identified in question 1? Why do you think so?
   a. The Bible
   b. Situational answer to prayer
   c. Advice of trusted friends
   d. Intuition
   e. A personal revelation from God
   f. Other _____

3. Why was Israel to *follow* the ark of the covenant in crossing the Jordan (Josh. 3:3-4, 10-11)?

4. What was the content of the Lord's message to Joshua (vv. 7-8)? What was the content of Joshua's message to the people (vv. 10-13)? How did they differ? How were they the same?

5. Why do you think Joshua didn't tell the people that God planned to exalt him in their eyes?

6. Describe the role of the priests who carried the ark (vv. 3-4, 8, 15-17).

7. If you had been an average Israelite following the ark that day, what would have been your reaction when each of these events took place?
   a. Walking toward the river from camp
   b. Seeing the priests step into the Jordan
   c. Seeing and hearing the river rise up in a mass
   d. Hurrying across the dry riverbed
   e. Looking from the other side as the river returned to its course

8. If you had lived in Jericho, what would have been your reaction to news of how Israel crossed the Jordan?

 ## Going Deeper

9. What past examples of God's faithfulness give you confidence to trust Him now?

10. When God blesses you, how can you honor Him? Give an example.

11. How might unbelievers observe God at work in your life and be drawn to Him?

♥ CARING TIME

The children of Israel were drawn together and unified by their shared experience of wandering in the wilderness and then crossing the Jordan River. God used this event and the ceremonies we will study in the next two lessons to prepare His people to accomplish a great work together. Our caring time activities can serve similar purposes. We have shared in the study of God's Word. Now we can share our hearts and lives with each other.

1. For which of the lesson principles do you most need to make a fresh application in your life?
   a. God honors faith, but He does not expect His children to operate on blind faith.
   b. God honors Christians who put Him first.
   c. God is still reaching out to lost people.

2. Specifically, what do you think you need to do to implement the principle you chose above?

3. How can we support you and hold you accountable for applying this principle in your life?

NEXT WEEK

Next week we look at how God instructed Israel to memorialize their miraculous crossing of the Jordan River. You may think it strange that they took time to consider the reaction of future generations to that achievement. This is one of those incidents that remind us that God's perspective is different from and far above ours. Which of His works in our lives should we remember as of great significance? The answer to this question will become much clearer as we investigate the memorial celebration by the Jordan.

LESSON 4

JOSHUA 3:1-17

3:1-17 For a people whose journey began with the crossing of the Red Sea, this event must have been a frightening flashback. While Pharaoh was no longer pursuing them, it was flood season and no less terrifying.

3:3 When you see the ark of the covenant. Following God instead of their fears, the people stepped into the river at the first sign of the ark's appearance. The ark of the covenant was a chest of acacia wood covered with gold. Its dimensions were approximately 45" long, 27" wide, and 27" high. Its lid was of solid gold. Two golden cherubim faced one another atop the lid (Ex. 25:10-22). In it were the stone tablets with the Ten Commandments, a jar of manna, and Aaron's rod that had miraculously budded (Heb. 9:4). The ark represented the presence of the Lord. *follow it.* In the typical marching order of the Israelite camp, the ark and other "holy things" were in the middle of the travel column (Num. 10:14-28, note v. 21).

3:4 for you haven't traveled this way before. Although prior generations got their feet wet in the Red Sea, this was a new miracle. They knew they would experience a similar outcome. But even the more experienced would have to rely on faith once more.

3:5 Consecrate yourselves . . . the LORD . . . wonders. Joshua's command was full of eager expectation in preparation for a great event. No doubt they polished their best utensils and readied their finest clothes. The people of Israel would meet with God tomorrow. They had to be ready, especially within their hearts.

3:7 I will be with you. Moses must have been a hard act to follow. Would Joshua do it right? Would others see the same courage in him that they had seen in Moses? God's reassuring presence was as much to encourage Joshua as it was to spur the people of Israel on to battle.

3:10 everything was completed. Seven people groups would oppose the Israelites' possession of the land. Those same seven groups would hear about the front-page miracle at the Jordan River.

3:12 choose 12 men. These men were to gather 12 large stones from the riverbed for a monument to be built on the other side of the river (4:2-3). There is more to share about these stones in lesson 5.

3:15 Jordan overflows its banks. That God arranged for the Israelites to cross the Jordan during the spring flood stage is no more surprising than the roundabout way He led them to Canaan in the first place. Sure, there was a direct route, just as the river would have been much less intimidating without the melting snow from Mount Hermon far to the north. However, less water may have required less faith. The Jordan may have been as much as 100 yards wide where Israel crossed.

3:16 Adam. A city near the place the Jabbok River emptied into the Jordan River from the east about 18 miles north of Jericho. Adam sat on the east side of the Jordan. Jericho lay inland on the west side.

3:17 firmly on dry ground. The completeness of God's miracle did not even allow for shallow puddles to remain. The priests took their posts in the middle of the river "on dry ground" and directed the Israelites across.

PERSONAL NOTES

THE FIASCO OF FORGETTING

LAST WEEK

Last week we looked at the faith of the priests who stepped into the raging Jordan River, and the humility of Joshua who gave all the credit for his accomplishments to the Lord. The priests carried the ark of the covenant into the water because they believed the Lord was with them and would fulfill His promise to stop the flow of the ferocious river. Joshua felt no need to puff himself up by taking credit for the deeds God enabled him to do. With attitudes like these at work among their leadership, Israel had great role models to follow and could expect great blessings from God.

ICEBREAKER

Memory plays an important role in anchoring our lives to their moorings. We draw our sense of purpose and stability from remembering how God has actively worked in and through our lives. When we remember where we have come from and how we got where we are, we maintain a proper perspective. We can make better sense of the present. The past also shows the trajectory of our lives and provides clues about where we might be headed.

1. If you went to the house or neighborhood where you grew up, which of these would you look for as a reminder of your boyhood?
   a. A tree you climbed in
   b. A yard or park you played ball in
   c. A room where you spent hours dreaming
   d. A creek or woods you explored
   e. Initials you carved in wood or stone
   f. A place where you achieved something great
   g. A cemetery representing a great loss
   h. Other _____

2. What family traditions or rituals surrounding holidays, birthdays, vacations, or other unique events do you remember from childhood?

3. What is your most treasured souvenir or keepsake? What does it represent to you?

Over 40 years earlier, when the children of Israel had crossed the Red Sea, they had left Egypt, the *land of bondage*. Now they had crossed over the Jordan River and stood on the threshold of Canaan, the promised *land of freedom*.

In order to enjoy this freedom, the Israelites were required to live up to some specific conditions that God had outlined for their benefit. Our Creator knows how quickly people forget and become self-absorbed. To ensure that Israel never forgot that He had redeemed them from slavery in Egypt, God gave them the Passover feast as a reminder. In order to keep them from forgetting the commandments He had given them at Mount Sinai, He provided the stone tablets on which He had written with His finger. Most recently, He had them set up memorial stones so they might never forget how He brought them mightily across the Jordan into the promised land.

Model for and Teach the Next Generation

[1] After the entire nation had finished crossing the Jordan, the Lord spoke to Joshua, [2] "Choose 12 men from the people, one man for each tribe, [3] and command them, 'Take 12 stones from this place in the middle of the Jordan where the priests' feet are standing, carry them with you, and set them down at the place where you spend the night.' "

[4] So Joshua summoned the 12 men selected from the Israelites, one man for each tribe, [5] and said to them, "Go across to the ark of the Lord your God in the middle of the Jordan. Each of you lift a stone onto his shoulder, one for each of the Israelite tribes, [6] so that this will be a sign among you. In the future, when your children ask you, 'What do these stones mean to you?' [7] you should tell them, 'The waters of the Jordan were cut off in front of the ark of the Lord's covenant. When it crossed the Jordan, the Jordan's waters were cut off.' Therefore these stones will always be a memorial for the Israelites."

[8] The Israelites did just as Joshua had commanded them. The 12 men took stones from the middle of the Jordan, one for each of the Israelite tribes, just as the Lord had told Joshua. They carried them to the camp and set them down there. [9] Joshua also set up 12 stones in the middle of the Jordan where the priests who carried the ark of the covenant were standing. The stones are there to this day.

[10] The priests carrying the ark continued standing in the middle of the Jordan until everything was completed that the Lord had commanded Joshua to tell the people, in keeping with all that Moses had

LESSON 5

commanded Joshua. The people hurried across, [11] and after everyone had finished crossing, the priests with the ark of the Lord crossed in the sight of the people. [12] The Reubenites, Gadites, and half the tribe of Manasseh went in battle formation in front of the Israelites, as Moses had instructed them. [13] About 40,000 equipped for war crossed to the plains of Jericho in the Lord's presence.

[14] On that day the Lord exalted Joshua in the sight of all Israel, and they revered him throughout his life, as they had revered Moses. [15] The Lord told Joshua, [16] "Command the priests who carry the ark of the testimony to come up from the Jordan."

[17] So Joshua commanded the priests, "Come up from the Jordan." [18] When the priests carrying the ark of the Lord's covenant came up from the middle of the Jordan, and their feet stepped out on solid ground, the waters of the Jordan resumed their course, flowing over all the banks as before.

[19] The people came up from the Jordan on the tenth day of the first month, and camped at Gilgal on the eastern limits of Jericho. [20] Then Joshua set up in Gilgal the 12 stones they had taken from the Jordan, [21] and he said to the Israelites, "When your children ask their fathers in the future, 'What is the meaning of these stones?' [22] you should tell your children, 'Israel crossed the Jordan on dry ground.' [23] For the Lord your God dried up the waters of the Jordan before you until you had crossed over, just as the Lord your God did to the Red Sea, which He dried up before us until we had crossed over. [24] This is so that all the people of the earth may know that the Lord's hand is mighty, and so that you may always fear the Lord your God."

Joshua 4:1-24

Principles to Live By

The placement of memorial stones at nearby Gilgal and in the middle of the Jordan River were both positive acts. Israel set up the monument at Gilgal in obedience to the Lord's command. It seems that Joshua erected the monument in the river as a spontaneous act of worship apart from any command of God. At the time, both memorials seemed destined to serve noble purposes for generations to come.

Tragically they did not. The historical lessons of the memorial stones of Joshua 4 are very negative ones. Let's see what happens when we fail to heed the past and forget the gracious and mighty acts of God on our behalf.

WHEN WE FAIL TO MODEL AND TEACH GOD'S WORD, IT ONLY
TAKES ONE GENERATION FOR TOTAL COLLAPSE TO TAKE PLACE.

Israel, God's own chosen people, failed to remind their children of
what God did at the Jordan River and in the conquest of the promised
land. No sooner had they settled into the land flowing with milk and
honey than their memories began to fade. Even the memorial stones at
Gilgal and in the middle of the river were forgotten by the majority in
Israel.

Many years had passed since Israel had crossed over Jordan and set up
the memorial stones in Gilgal. God had given them victory after victory.
After years of bondage and wilderness wanderings, they had settled
into the land and enjoyed the freedom of having a place to live in peace
and plenty. Then something unbelievable happened. One of the most
heartbreaking and sobering statements in all of Scripture is recorded in
Judges 2.

The book of Judges reads, "Joshua son of Nun, the servant of the
Lord, died at the age of 110. ... That whole generation was also gathered
to their ancestors. After them another generation rose up who did not
know the Lord or the works He had done for Israel" (Judg. 2:8, 10).

It may be difficult to comprehend how such a change could take
place in Israel in such a short period of time. However, think for a minute
about what has happened in modern Western culture in the last 50 or
60 years. Our whole value system has changed, dramatically affecting the
family unit and, in turn, the moral fabric of our entire society. When we
ceased to reflect God's values in our homes, it only took one generation for
spiritual degeneration to take place.

PRINCIPLE 2

THE BIBLE TEACHES THAT AS MEN WE HAVE A TREMENDOUS
RESPONSIBILITY TO TAKE THE LEAD IN TEACHING BIBLICAL VALUES
TO OUR CHILDREN.

Moses had charged Israel, "These words that I am giving you today
are to be in your heart. Repeat them to your children. Talk about them
when you sit in your house and when you walk along the road, when you
lie down and when you get up. Bind them as a sign on your hand and let
them be a symbol on your forehead. Write them on the doorposts of your
house and on your gates.

"When the Lord your God brings you into the land He swore to your
fathers Abraham, Isaac, and Jacob that He would give you—a [land with]

large and beautiful cities that you did not build, houses full of every good thing that you did not fill [them with], wells dug that you did not dig, and vineyards and olive groves that you did not plant—and when you eat and are satisfied, be careful not to forget the Lord who brought you out of the land of Egypt, out of the place of slavery" (Deut. 6:6-12).

The fathers of Israel failed their children, and they forgot the Lord. What will our children remember about us? Will they remember only beautiful homes, big-screen television sets, DVD players, computer games, fast cars, vacation homes, speedboats, open-ended allowances, and all the frantic efforts we put into accumulating and maintaining all this stuff?

Though these material "things" are not wrong in themselves, will our children remember any spiritual lessons and experiences marked by memorial stones of family traditions and celebrations? It's never too late to start building a culture of spiritual values in your home. Whether your children are small or grown, they should experience your home as a place where conversation honors God, where fathers treat mothers and children with love and respect, where entertainment is wholesome, where faith in God looks to the future with optimism, and gratitude toward God remembers what He's done in the past, and where God's Word is held up as the standard for all of life

QUESTIONS FOR INTERACTION

1. What is the greatest display of God's power on your behalf that you ever experienced?

2. How do you memorialize the events you identified in question 1?

3. How do you suppose the 12 Israelites felt when Joshua ordered them back into the riverbed to gather the memorial stones (Josh. 4:4-5)?

4. Why do you suppose Joshua set up 12 stones in the center of the river, even though the Lord hadn't commanded him to do so (v. 9)?

5. How did the Lord exalt Joshua in the eyes of Israel (v. 14)?

6. What was the function within Israel of the memorial stones the people set up in Gilgal (vv. 6-7, 19-23)?

7. What was the function among the nations of the memorial stones the people set up in Gilgal (v. 24)?

8. Refer to questions 1 and 2 again. What other events in your Christian life would be beneficial for you to memorialize in some way?

9. How might you celebrate the most significant of these events?

GOING DEEPER

10. How can fathers lead their families in celebrating "spiritual birthdays," holidays, and other special events and spiritual milestones?

11. What might we do to mark the transition from childhood to manhood or womanhood for our children?

12. What can we resolve to do to prevent the next generation from forgetting the Lord and His mighty deeds?

13. How can we help the next generation to know God personally and experience first-hand the blessings and power of a Christ-centered life?

CARING TIME

Most men find it a little intimidating to think about planning celebrations. God, however, holds us accountable for teaching the next generation, whether they are our children or the children of our church, community, or sports team. Remember, many of us have a ready helper in our wives if we would just begin to lead. Let's consider some of our responsibilities in this area.

1. Which of these action steps do you need to work on first?
    a. Display and elevate Scripture in my home
    b. Talk about God's desires and pray for His direction when making decisions within my family
    c. Convey to my children (or children I influence) respect and reverence for God
    d. Begin to establish spiritually-focused celebrations in my family for key holidays and milestones
    e. Seek out opportunities to expose my children to experiencing God, His heart, and His power first-hand
    f. Other _____

2. How can we support you and hold you accountable for working on this action step?

3. Who are some other men we should encourage to join in our small group? How should we go about inviting them?

NEXT WEEK

Next week we review the final preparation God put His people through before sending them against the fortress city of Jericho. The Lord did not ask the army to drill harder or learn the use of new weapons. God was not primarily concerned about the military readiness of Israel. His first concern was about the spiritual purity of Israel's army. Almost under the very walls of Jericho, the Lord disabled the entire fighting force of Israel for several days by requiring their circumcision. The army of Israel consecrated itself to the Lord so it could be His instrument to purge Canaan of the corruption caused by its wicked inhabitants.

SCRIPTURE NOTES

JOSHUA 4:1-24

4:3 from this place in the middle of the Jordan. As a symbol of their great faith and God's greater miracle, a select group representing each of the 12 tribes of Israel took stones from the deepest part of the river and set them aside for a memorial.

4:6 a sign among you. Bumper stickers. Patches. Flags. People are drawn to symbols as expressions of what is important and valued. To the Israelites, this stone monument would help families remember God's faithfulness for generations to come.

4:9 The stones are there to this day. The stones still remained at the time the book of Joshua was written, not at the present. Some scholars think this could mean as many as 800 years later.

4:13 40,000. This was less than the number of fighting men recorded in Numbers for Reuben or Gad alone (Num. 1:21, 25). This figure is likely a total of representatives from the two and one-half tribes involved. The others stayed in Transjordan to protect their families, settlements, and possessions.

4:14 the LORD exalted Joshua. At this time and in this way the Lord fulfilled the promise He made to Joshua a chapter earlier (3:7).

4:19 Gilgal. Gilgal means "A circle [of stones]." The name may derive from the monument of stones set up there at this time. This camp became the military headquarters for Joshua's entire campaign against the land of Canaan (Josh. 6:11; 10:7; 14:6). Saul would later be crowned the first king of Israel at Gilgal (1 Sam. 11:15). **on the eastern limits of Jericho.** The administrative control of Jericho extended the two miles into the countryside to the vicinity of Gilgal.

4:23 God dried up the waters . . . before you. The story the Israelites would tell future generations had one moral: God delivers. It was not about the amount of people's faith or the size of the river. The story was about God Himself. **just as . . . the Red Sea.** God wanted the parallels between the earlier miracle He had performed through Moses and the present miracle He did through Joshua to be obvious to the Israelites and all other observers.

4:24 all the people of the earth. Although this miracle was specific to the Israelites at that time, God's fame would be spread throughout the world as a result. The timeless truths the event symbolized would be shared for generations.

PERSONAL NOTES

RECAPTURED ALLEGIANCE

LAST WEEK

Last week we started looking at how important it is to remember what God has done for us. God directed the Israelites to erect a stone memorial they could use to teach succeeding generations how He had brought them miraculously across the Jordan River on dry ground. We examined in the book of Judges how Israel failed to carry out this generational mission (2:8-10). In only a single generation, commitment to God disappeared. This week we continue the theme of remembrance by looking at repeating sacramental, memorial acts that form a crucial part of the communal life of God's people.

ICEBREAKER

It's amazing how naturally people assign meaning to objects. The flag stands for the country. A rabbit's foot means good luck. A child's blanket is security. We do the same thing with events. Birthdays, anniversaries, holidays, and family traditions give rhythm and meaning to life.

1. Which "rite of passage" marked your entrance into adulthood?
    a. Your own car
    b. Your driver's license
    c. Your confirmation
    d. Your first drink or cigarette
    e. Your high school graduation
    f. Your first job
    g. Your marriage
    h. Other _____

2. What are some foods that you associate so strongly with certain events that you cannot eat them without thinking of the events?

3. What's the weirdest ritual you ever participated in?

Once the Israelites had crossed the Jordan River into Canaan, they were exposed to great danger. The flooded stream was behind them now. Retreat was impossible, barring another miracle. The fortress-city of Jericho loomed little more than two miles from their camp at Gilgal. Perhaps the king of Jericho had sounded the alarm after the spies escaped and summoned a Canaanite force to repel the invaders.

What would God direct Joshua to do? Would Israel attack Jericho immediately? Would they fashion elaborate defensive measures around Gilgal? Would they scout any enemy troop movements to find out how the Canaanites were preparing to resist them?

God did none of those things. His ways are not our ways and His thoughts are beyond our comprehension. He was more concerned about the spiritual preparation of His people than their military readiness. He knew that if their hearts were turned to Him in devotion, He could better direct them in the battles ahead.

Set Apart to the Lord

[1] When all the Amorite kings across the Jordan to the west and all the Canaanite kings near the sea heard how the Lord had dried up the waters of the Jordan before the Israelites until they had crossed over, they lost heart and their courage failed because of the Israelites.

[2] At that time the Lord said to Joshua, "Make flint knives and circumcise the Israelite men again." [3] So Joshua made flint knives and circumcised the Israelite men at Gibeath-haaraloth. [4] This is the reason Joshua circumcised [them]: All the people who came out of Egypt who were males—all the men of war—had died in the wilderness along the way after they had come out of Egypt. [5] Though all the people who came out were circumcised, none of the people born in the wilderness along the way were circumcised after they had come out of Egypt. [6] For the Israelites wandered in the wilderness 40 years until all the nation's men of war who came out of Egypt had died off because they did not obey the Lord. So the Lord vowed never to let them see the land He had sworn to their fathers to give us, a land flowing with milk and honey. [7] Joshua raised up their sons in their place; it was these he circumcised. They were still uncircumcised, since they had not been circumcised along the way. [8] After the entire nation had been circumcised, they stayed where they were in the camp until they recovered. [9] The Lord then said to Joshua, "Today I have rolled away the disgrace of Egypt from you." Therefore, that place has been called Gilgal to this day.

[10] While the Israelites camped at Gilgal on the plains of Jericho, they

kept the Passover on the evening of the fourteenth day of the month. ¹¹ The day after Passover they ate unleavened bread and roasted grain from the produce of the land. ¹² And the day after they ate from the produce of the land, the manna ceased. Since there was no more manna for the Israelites, they ate from the crops of the land of Canaan that year.

¹³ When Joshua was near Jericho, he looked up and saw a man standing in front of him with a drawn sword in His hand. Joshua approached Him and asked, "Are You for us or for our enemies?"

¹⁴ "Neither," He replied. "I have now come as commander of the Lord's army."

Then Joshua bowed with his face to the ground in worship and asked Him, "What does my Lord want to say to His servant?"

¹⁵ The commander of the Lord's army said to Joshua, "Remove the sandals from your feet, for the place where you are standing is holy." And Joshua did so.

Joshua 5:1-15

PRINCIPLES TO LIVE BY

When God commanded Joshua to remember His acts of love and grace by means of circumcision and the Passover celebration, it was not something new in Israel's history. God had regularly used ritual and ceremony as a means to direct people's attention to Himself. He continues to provide rites of remembrance for His children even in New Testament days. God knows full well that our memories need to be stimulated with regular reminders, and He has factored that into His great plan for the church and the individual's life of faith.

PRINCIPLE 1

WE NEED THE REMEMBRANCE OF BAPTISM LEST WE FORGET THAT WE HAVE DIED WITH CHRIST AND BEEN RESURRECTED TO A NEW LIFE IN HIM.

When the new generation of Israelites under Joshua's command entered the promised land, the Lord instructed that all the men of Israel be circumcised (Josh. 5:2). Circumcision identified Israel as God's special covenant people. The Lord had instituted this rite when He first called Abraham out of paganism and covenanted to make him a great nation, provide him with a multitude of offspring, make his name great, give him special land for his descendants, and bless the entire world through him (Gen. 12:1-7).

By obeying the Lord's command to be circumcised, the generation that would finally conquer and take possession of the promised land of Canaan reaffirmed their covenant relation with the Lord. They also made a clean break with their past. In the act of circumcision God "rolled away the disgrace of Egypt" from His people (Josh. 5:9).

Baptism fills a similar function in the lives of Christian believers. It's a mark of the new covenant that indicates believers have become part of the body of Christ (1 Cor. 12:13). It visually portrays that we have died with Christ and been resurrected to "a new way of life" (Rom. 6:4-8). Our salvation is by grace alone through faith alone (Rom. 5:1-2; Eph. 2:8-9). But through baptism we identify with the death and resurrection of Jesus and we witness this fact to unbelievers. Baptism appeals to unbelievers to cross over from death into life through faith in the One who died and rose again for them.

PRINCIPLE 2

WE NEED THE REMEMBRANCE OF THE LORD'S SUPPER LEST WE FORGET THAT HIS BODY WAS BROKEN AND HIS BLOOD SHED FOR THE SINS OF THE WORLD.

Just before God delivered the children of Israel from Egyptian bondage, He instituted the Passover meal as a remembrance of their salvation. Every aspect of the meal represents some aspect of their past bondage or their deliverance. At the heart of this remembrance was the flawless Passover lamb whose shed blood had been used to save their firstborn sons from the angel of death (Ex. 12:5, 7, 13). As circumcision reminded Israel of the covenant God had made with them, the Passover reminded them of their redemption that fitted them for the blessings of that covenant.

For Christians the memorial event involving food is called communion or the Lord's Supper. Jesus instituted this "remembrance" while He was observing the Passover with His disciples on the evening before His crucifixion. As He broke the bread that evening and drank the cup with His followers, He demonstrated how His body would be bruised and His blood shed for the sins of the world. "Do this," He said, "in remembrance of Me" (Luke 22:19). Paul elaborated on Christ's words in his first letter to the Corinthians when he wrote, "For as often as you eat this bread and drink the cup, you proclaim the Lord's death until He comes" (1 Cor. 11:26).

QUESTIONS FOR INTERACTION

1. Which of these best describes your baptism?
   a. I hear I was a baby.
   b. I was a distracted boy trying to remember what I had been told to do.
   c. I was just doing what all my friends were doing.
   d. I was a new believer excited to demonstrate my faith in Christ.
   e. I had been a believer for some time and wanted to obey Christ.
   f. Other _____.

2. When you participate in the Lord's Supper, what do you personally remember when you eat the bread? When you drink the cup?

3. Why did the Israelites have time to prepare themselves spiritually before they would have to do battle (Josh. 5:1)?

4. Why did most of the male population of Israel need to be circumcised (vv. 2-7)?

5. What did God want this mass circumcision to communicate and signify to the invading Israelites (vv. 8-9)?

6. How did celebrating the Passover at this time reinforce the significance of the circumcision ceremony?

7. What was the significance to the Israelites that God had stopped the daily supply of manna now that they were in Canaan (vv. 11-12)?

8. What would it mean to Joshua to know that the real commander of the Lord's army was a supernatural being (vv. 13-15)?

9. What made that patch of ground just outside Jericho holy (v. 15)?

10. How might you prepare yourself spiritually before major events in your life?

 GOING DEEPER

11. How can you keep the memory of your baptism from becoming stale and meaningless?

12. How can you keep your observance of the Lord's Supper from becoming routine and dull?

13. How can we prepare our children for baptism or help them remember and appreciate their baptism?

14. How can we help our children participate more meaningfully in communion?

CARING TIME

A whole generation of Israelite men prepared themselves to be the army of the Lord against the Canaanites. They must have had an unusual sense of unity and purpose as the Passover festival ended and the battle for Jericho loomed in their thoughts. We also would do well to fully utilize those reminders that God gives us to focus our hearts and energies on His goals for us.

1. If any men in our group have not been baptized, what kind of encouragement would you give them?

2. How can we better use the baptism services of our church to witness to unbelieving friends?

3. What do you find most meaningful about communion services? Now, let's pray that God will powerfully use our times of communion to draw us closer to one another, and together set us apart as warriors for His battle.

LESSON 6

NEXT WEEK

Next week we follow the Israelite army in its curious assault on the walled city of Jericho. It's a good thing the commander of the Lord's army revealed himself to Joshua at the end of Joshua 5, because the strategy the Lord had in mind for capturing Jericho might otherwise have been hard to believe. The bottom line was that if Israel would obey the Lord's unusual directions, He would knock down the city's walls for them. The army could then rush in upon a stunned, defenseless people. Joshua believed the Lord and obeyed without hesitation. His victory is one of the best-loved stories in the Bible because of the dramatic way in which God brought victory.

SCRIPTURE NOTES

JOSHUA 5:1-15

5:1-12 Like a family resuming family dinners after a particularly busy period of scattered priorities, the Israelites reintroduced two important traditions. The new family members were circumcised and the entire group celebrated Passover together.

5:1 Amorite. The Amorites were an ancient people by Joshua's time. Their glory days had been in the time of Abraham. The name meant something like "Westerner" or "mountain-dweller." Sometimes Amorite is used as a synonym for Canaanite, but not in this passage. Amorites also lived east of the Jordan. Israel had already defeated the Amorite king Sihon before crossing into Canaan (Num. 21:21-31).

5:2 flint knives. The Bronze Age had long since begun, but ancient implements seem to have been preferred for ceremonial purposes. Moses' son had been circumcised with a flint knife more than 40 years earlier as Moses prepared to confront Pharaoh in Egypt (Ex. 4:25).

5:6 wandered in the wilderness 40 years. The Lord waited for an entire disobedient generation to die off before bringing His people to the promised land.

5:9 Gilgal. Gilgal sounds like the Hebrew word "to roll." Joshua provides two possible explanations for this place name. The 12 stones from the Jordan were rolled into a circle (4:19) or the disgrace of Egypt was rolled away. This camp became the military headquarters for Joshua's entire campaign against the promised land (6:11; 10:7; 14:6). Saul would later be crowned the first king of Israel at Gilgal (1 Sam 11:15).

5:10 kept the Passover. This was the third time the Israelites would celebrate Passover together. The first time was before their exodus from Egypt (Ex. 12). The second time was at Sinai, where they received the Commandments (Num. 9:1-5). Now they observed Passover at Gilgal.

5:11 produce of the land. For the first time, the Israelites were able to enjoy the bounty of their land.

5:12 manna. A sweet bread that had appeared as white flakes on the ground when the dew evaporated each morning (except for Sabbaths) for 40 years (Ex. 16:14, 31). When the Israelites crossed the Jordan, they crossed into a new era of God's provision. No longer dependent on manna, they were able to further stake their claim on Canaan by enjoying its fruit.

5:13-15 for us or for our enemies. Jericho would be no ordinary battle. The stranger's appearance at its onset is a further reminder that the Israelites were fighting a battle the Lord had already won for them. This spiritual encounter set the tone for the entire record of the battle of Jericho.

5:13 a man standing in front. Regardless of whether the man was an angel on a mission, Christ pre incarnate, or God the Father in human form, the encounter had to be inspiring for Joshua. A supernatural army's presence, in addition to his faithful men, bolstered his confidence.

5:14 I have now come as commander of the Lord's army. Joshua submitted in reverence to this supernaturally superior officer, whether angel or God Himself.

5:15 the place where you are standing is holy. Moses received the same command at the burning bush (Ex. 3:2, 5). Now, Joshua realized his own encounter with the Lord had brought him to a holy place.

PERSONAL NOTES

A RADICAL WRECKING BALL

LAST WEEK

Last week we completed our examination of the way God prepared His people for the invasion of Canaan. The Lord interrupted any military preparations to ready the children of Israel spiritually. To do this He took them back to the roots of their faith. He called on Joshua to circumcise all the males who had been born during the 40 years since Israel left Egypt. This action reaffirmed that Israel was the covenant people of God. They also celebrated the Passover to remember as a nation that they were the people God had redeemed from Egyptian slavery. Only after the Israelites fully grasped who they were and aligned themselves in right relation with God, were they ready to fight the first battle in Canaan—the battle of Jericho.

 ## ICEBREAKER

The battle of Jericho served as a clear warning to the Canaanites that this was no ordinary army invading their land. They had been bothered by rumors of a long-ago, far-away miracle at the Red Sea and a right-here, right-now miracle at the Jordan River. Now they were about to become petrified by the events that would unfold at Jericho.

No battle is a pretty thing. Every fight involving physical violence affects the hearts and minds of everyone in it.

1. When you were a teenager, what was your experience with fighting?
    a.   I got in a lot of fights.
    b.   A bully picked on me.
    c.   I got in one fight, and it cured me of solving problems that way.
    d.   I was a peacemaker.
    e.   I was not a fighter; I spent a lot of time running from trouble.
    f.   My parents would have killed me if I got in a fight.
    g.   I was the bully who picked on nerds.
    h.   Other _____.

2. How did you feel about the fights you were in or witnessed as a teenager?

3. What experience, if any, have you had as an adult with fighting (in the military or other settings)?

BIBLICAL FOUNDATION

The children of Israel had entered the land of Canaan. It was a dream come true! God had once again demonstrated His great power by stopping the flow of the flooded Jordan River. He had reminded Israel of His unconditional covenant with them through the rite of circumcision. He had also reminded them of His grace in delivering them from Egyptian bondage by means of the Passover celebration. Israel stood poised to take the promised land through military advancement. The city of Jericho was, by God's direct command, to be Israel's first target. And, it would fall!

"The LORD has given you the city."

[1] Now Jericho was strongly fortified because of the Israelites—no one leaving or entering. [2] The Lord said to Joshua, "Look, I have handed Jericho, its king, and its fighting men over to you. [3] March around the city with all the men of war, circling the city one time. Do this for six days. [4] Have seven priests carry seven ram's-horn trumpets in front of the ark. But on the seventh day, march around the city seven times, while the priests blow the trumpets. [5] When there is a prolonged blast of the horn and you hear its sound, have all the people give a mighty shout. Then the city wall will collapse, and the people will advance, each man straight ahead." . . .

[8] After Joshua had spoken to the people, seven priests carrying seven trumpets before the Lord moved forward and blew the trumpets; the ark of the Lord's covenant followed them. [9] While the trumpets were blowing, the armed troops went in front of the priests who blew the trumpets, and the rear guard went behind the ark. [10] But Joshua had commanded the people: "Do not shout or let your voice be heard. Don't let one word come out of your mouth until the time I say, 'Shout!' Then you are to shout." [11] So the ark of the Lord was carried around the city, circling it once. They returned to the camp and spent the night there. ... [14] On the second day they marched around the city once and returned to the camp. They did this for six days.

[15] Early on the seventh day, they started at dawn and marched around the city seven times in the same way. That was the only day they marched around the city seven times. [16] After the seventh time, the priests blew the trumpets, and Joshua said to the people, "Shout! For the Lord has given you the city. [17] But the city and everything in it are

set apart to the Lord for destruction. Only Rahab the prostitute and everyone with her in the house will live, because she hid the men we sent. [18] But keep yourselves from the things set apart, or you will be set apart for destruction. If you take any of those things, you will set apart the camp of Israel for destruction and bring disaster on it. [19] For all the silver and gold, and the articles of bronze and iron, are dedicated to the Lord and must go into the Lord's treasury."

[20] So the people shouted, and the trumpets sounded. When they heard the blast of the trumpet, the people gave a great shout, and the wall collapsed. The people advanced into the city, each man straight ahead, and they captured the city. [21] They completely destroyed everything in the city with the sword—every man and woman, both young and old, and every ox, sheep, and donkey.

[22] Joshua said to the two men who had scouted the land, "Go to the prostitute's house and bring the woman out of there, and all who are with her, just as you promised her." [23] So the young men who had scouted went in and brought out Rahab and her father, mother, brothers, and all who belonged to her. They brought out her whole family and settled them outside the camp of Israel.

[24] They burned up the city and everything in it, but they put the silver and gold and the articles of bronze and iron into the treasury of the Lord's house. [25] But Joshua spared Rahab the prostitute, her father's household, and all who belonged to her, because she hid the men Joshua had sent to spy on Jericho, and she lives in Israel to this day. …

[27] And the Lord was with Joshua, and his fame spread throughout the land.

Joshua 6:1-5, 8-11, 15-25, 27

Principles to Live By

The first battle Israel fought in Canaan served several purposes. The battle of Jericho strengthened the confidence and resolve of the army of Israel for the long campaign ahead. Jericho firmly established that God was in control of the conquest of the promised land. Jericho also served as one more powerful warning to the other Canaanite cities, "Your turn is coming; watch out! Israel was on the march under the command of the living God.

With each of His mighty deeds God was saying, "Repent! Repent! Repent! Turn from your wicked ways, your immoralities, your false gods, your child sacrifices, and your many other evil deeds. If you do, I'll preserve you as I did Rahab the prostitute and her entire family." How would the Canaanites respond?

Somehow the people of Jericho believed they could protect themselves from the God of Israel behind man-made walls. They ignored the fact that those walls of stone were just as much subject to God's power as the waters of the Red Sea and the Jordan River. Obviously, if God could control and manipulate natural phenomena, He could destroy man-made structures and thwart bows and arrows with no problem.

Still today, men and women who do not know God and who are blinded by their self-centered lifestyles and pagan religions hide within their unbelief and feel secure. They feel shielded from God by the apparent permanence of the physical world, by the social structures they live within, and by their arguments against the existence of the God of the Bible.

Peter reminds scoffers who think judgment will never come: "Don't let this one thing escape you: with the Lord one day is like 1,000 years, and 1,000 years like one day. The Lord does not delay His promise, as some understand delay, but is patient with you, not wanting any to perish, but all to come to repentance" (2 Pet. 3:8-9).

PRINCIPLE 2

GOD IS STILL PATIENT AND LONG-SUFFERING WITH PEOPLE WHO REJECT HIM.

Jesus Christ is still waiting for people to turn to Him. In His mysterious and sovereign way, He is delaying His return to earth because He desires that all people be saved. Obviously, not all will turn to Him, but some will, just as Rahab and her family did. Jesus taught that the road leading to destruction is wide, and many follow that road. He also explained that the road leading to eternal life is narrow, and few follow that path (Matt. 7:13-14). The people of Jericho exemplified those who choose the wide path. Rahab and her family certainly exemplified those who choose the narrow path.

What about you? Have you personally received Jesus Christ as your Savior from sin and eternal death? Don't put off this important decision any longer. Invite Him into your life and receive His forgiveness today. Pray this prayer with sincerity and He promises to accept you as His child and give you eternal life with Him:

LESSON 7

Father, I have sinned. My sins may not be as bad as those of the ancient Canaanites, but I know they separate me from You. Thank You for sending Jesus to die for my sins. I receive Him as my personal Savior and my Lord. Thank You for accepting me, forgiving me, saving me, and giving me eternal life. Amen.

PRINCIPLE 3

GOD USES PEOPLE TO REACH PEOPLE.

One of the reasons God had Israel march around Jericho for seven days was His overall plan for reaching out to and offering redemption and newness of life to all people and nations. Israel was God's chosen means, in Old Testament days, to convey *to all nations* His existence, His sovereignty, His righteousness, and His holiness. He chose Israel to bear the message that He was willing to save all those who would truly call upon Him, whether Jews or Gentile.

We have the same responsibility today as Christians. There are five areas we should be involved in as colaborers with God in His missionary strategy. *Being*: Living out in the church what Jesus commanded and prayed for in John's Gospel—especially love and unity—will serve as a dynamic bridge to the world around us. *Going:* We all must be involved in outreach to those around us, and available to become missionaries if God calls us to. *Sending and Giving:* We are to commission and support those whom God calls to share the gospel with people far away. *Praying:* We need to pray fervently for missionaries near and far who are sharing with people the life-giving message of forgiveness and hope found in Christ and His sacrifice for them.

QUESTIONS FOR INTERACTION

1. What about your life is most likely to draw people's attention to Jesus Christ?
    a. The ordinary things I do.
    b. The ordinary things I say.
    c. The out-of-the-ordinary things I do.
    d. The out-of-the-ordinary things I say.
    e. Other _____.

2. How do you react to the idea that people around you can be uncomfortable knowing that you are a committed Christ-follower?

3. How do the instructions the Lord gave Joshua for the Jericho campaign show that He truly was the commander of the army of Israel (Josh. 6:2-5)?

4. Who from the Israelite camp marched around Jericho each day (v. 3)?

5. Describe what the scene must have been like, including sights and sounds, of the Israelite "assault" on Jericho (vv. 8-11).

6. What do you imagine the residents of Jericho were thinking on the seventh day when the army of Israel kept on circling their city (v. 15)?

7. Why might God have wanted the first city in Canaan set apart completely to Him for destruction (vv. 17-19)?

8. This is a familiar story, but share any new insights you discovered about the defeat and destruction of Jericho (vv. 20-27).

9. When the battle of Jericho was over, how should the Israelites have felt about God, about Joshua, and about the Canaanites?

10. Why are there some things God wants us to do His way instead of ours?

GOING DEEPER

11. Among the unbelievers who watch your life, who tends to scoff at your faith and who seems interested?

12. With which unbelievers do you need to exercise more patience and long-suffering, even as God does?

13. To become more involved in God's missionary strategy, where do you need to focus more attention right now? Being? Going? Sending? Giving? Praying?

14. How can you increase the amount of contact you have with unbelievers in your life who need to hear about Jesus?

CARING TIME

As individuals and as a group, we need to reflect the Lord's heart of compassion and mercy for unbelievers. God desires that all people come to know His Son as Savior, and we should too. Sometimes our attention gets turned to other areas of life, and we forget how important it is to God that everyone hears about Jesus and has opportunity to experience forgiveness, salvation, and new life in Christ.

1. How can we use this group and other programs of our church to reach out to unbelieving family and friends?

2. What social or recreational activities might we add to our group's agenda in order to reach out to unbelievers?

3. What service project could our group undertake to reach out to needy people in our community, sharing Christ as we meet real-life needs?

Next Week

Next week we will discover that not every Israelite obeyed the Lord completely at Jericho. Hidden sin led to severe consequences for the army of Israel in its next attack on a Canaanite city. God refused to let His people advance another mile into the promised land until they dealt harshly with rebellion in their own ranks. Jesus expressed a similar attitude toward sin when He said, "If your right eye causes you to sin, gouge it out and throw it away. For it is better that you lose one of the parts of your body than for your whole body to be thrown into hell" (Matt. 5:29). Though Jesus was using hyperbole, He was definitely teaching all of us how odious sin is and how important it is to deal with it in our lives before it ultimately destroys us.

Scripture Notes

Joshua 6:1-5, 8-11, 15-25, 27

6:1 Jericho was strongly fortified. The story of Israel's miraculous crossing apparently preceded them and terrified the inhabitants of Jericho. Inside two layers of thick walls, the citizens of Jericho awaited their fate.

6:3 March around the city . . . one time. Swords ready? Check! Ladders ready? Check! Shields ready? Check! Joshua's battle checklist surely never included merely marching around the walls of Jericho. However, his response was not a question. It was obedience.

6:4 ram's-horn trumpets. Typically, priests used these "jubilee trumpets" in religious ceremonies to announce the presence of the Lord.

6:5 give a mighty shout. The terrified and bewildered inhabitants inside Jericho would be stunned by the voices of tens of thousands of warriors, not to mention the roar of their crumbling walls.

6:8-14 Don't let one word come out of your mouth. Perhaps this was an additional guard against discouragement or negative comments since it was a particularly strange strategy for war.

6:17 set apart to the LORD for destruction. To be "set apart" in this case, when God was speaking of cities under His personal judgment, meant that these were to be completely destroyed. Much like a burnt offering, the entire city of Jericho was to be set aside as a sacrifice.

6:18 destruction. Whenever the Israelites did not obey God's command to destroy the contents of a city, disastrous consequences followed. The high stakes involved in disobedience would make sure Israel stayed pure among a pagan people.

6:25 Rahab . . . she lives in Israel to this day. Rahab's family and future were redeemed due to her fateful encounter with the spies. Apparently, she converted from her pagan ways and worshiped among the Israelites.

PERSONAL NOTES

THE TRAP OF LUST & SELFISHNESS

LAST WEEK

Last week we looked at the amazing story of the battle of Jericho. We saw how God took command of the army of Israel and issued very specific instructions through Joshua for an unorthodox assault on the Canaanite stronghold. Israel marched around the city with their mouths shut every day for six days. Priests blew ceremonial trumpets as they carried the ark of the covenant around the city with the troops. On the seventh day they circled the city seven times, shouted at the top of their voices, and the walls of Jericho collapsed. The Israelites rushed into the city, slaughtered its inhabitants, burned all the buildings, and placed all precious metals in the treasury of the tabernacle of God. It was a great victory! Now, we'll discover darkness and sin buried inside this shining victory.

ICEBREAKER

They (whoever "they" are) say a man's character is revealed by what he does when no one is watching. That's because no temptations are stronger than those we think we can yield to and yet never be found out. We struggled with this as boys when we walked by cookie jars. As adults we know how important it is to do the right thing, even when no one would ever know what we chose. However, knowing what's right doesn't make it easy to do right. The pull of temptation can be very strong.

1. When you were a boy, what gift did you most want for Christmas that you never got?

2. When you were young, what did you get caught at that you were sure you were going to get away with?

3. How did you feel about getting caught in question 2?

BIBLICAL FOUNDATION

The conquest of Jericho was a great victory for Joshua and the armies of Israel. From a human point of view, there was no way to explain the event. It was indeed another fantastic miracle, equal in intensity, drama, and divine significance to the Red Sea crossing and Israel's entrance into Canaan through the Jordan River.

Jericho was the first city to fall under the judgment of God. The next would be Ai, another Canaanite city that lay about 10 miles west of Jericho. Whatever fear and uncertainties the children of Israel may have felt when they first approached Jericho were replaced with abounding self-confidence. They were totally unprepared for what happened after that.

Disobedience, Defeat, and Death

¹ The Israelites, however, were unfaithful regarding the things set apart for destruction. Achan son of Carmi, son of Zabdi, son of Zerah, of the tribe of Judah, took some of what was set apart, and the Lord's anger burned against the Israelites.

² Joshua sent men from Jericho to Ai, which is near Beth-aven, east of Bethel, and told them, "Go up and scout the land." So the men went up and scouted Ai.

³ After returning to Joshua they reported to him, "Don't send all the people, but send about 2,000 or 3,000 men to attack Ai. Since the people of Ai are so few, don't wear out all our people there." ⁴ So about 3,000 men went up there, but they fled from the men of Ai. ⁵ The men of Ai struck down about 36 of them and chased them from outside the gate to the quarries, striking them down on the descent. As a result, the people's hearts melted and became like water.

⁶ Then Joshua tore his clothes and fell before the ark of the Lord with his face to the ground until evening, as did the elders of Israel; they all put dust on their heads. ⁷ "Oh, Lord God," Joshua said, "why did You ever bring these people across the Jordan to hand us over to the Amorites for our destruction? If only we had been content to remain on the other side of the Jordan! ⁸ What can I say, Lord, now that Israel has turned its back [and run] from its enemies? ⁹ When the Canaanites and all who live in the land hear about this, they will surround us and wipe out our name from the earth. Then what will You do about Your great name?"

¹⁰ The Lord then said to Joshua, "Stand up! Why are you on the ground? ¹¹ Israel has sinned. They have violated My covenant that I appointed for them. They have taken some of what was set apart. They have stolen, deceived, and put [the things] with their own belongings. ¹² This is why the Israelites cannot stand against their enemies. They will turn their backs [and run] from their enemies, because they have been set apart for destruction. I will no longer be with you unless you remove from you what is set apart.

13 "Go and consecrate the people. Tell them to consecrate themselves tomorrow, for this is what the Lord, the God of Israel, says, 'There are among you, Israel, things set apart. You will not be able to stand against your enemies until you remove what is set apart. 14 In the morning you must present yourselves tribe by tribe. The tribe the Lord selects is to come forward clan by clan. The clan the Lord selects is to come forward family by family. The family the Lord selects is to come forward man by man. 15 The one who is caught with the things set apart must be burned, along with everything he has, because he has violated the Lord's covenant and committed an outrage in Israel.' "

16 Joshua got up early the next morning. He had Israel come forward tribe by tribe, and the tribe of Judah was selected. 17 He had the clans of Judah come forward, and the Zerahite clan was selected. He had the Zerahite clan come forward by heads of families, and Zabdi was selected. 18 He then had Zabdi's family come forward man by man, and Achan son of Carmi, son of Zabdi, son of Zerah, of the tribe of Judah, was selected.

19 So Joshua said to Achan, "My son, give glory to the Lord, the God of Israel, and make a confession to Him. I urge you, tell me what you have done. Don't hide anything from me."

20 Achan replied to Joshua, "It is true. I have sinned against the Lord, the God of Israel. This is what I did: 21 When I saw among the spoils a beautiful cloak from Babylon, 200 silver shekels, and a bar of gold weighing 50 shekels, I coveted them and took them. You can see for yourself. They are concealed in the ground inside my tent, with the money under the cloak." 22 So Joshua sent messengers who ran to the tent, and there was the cloak, concealed in his tent, with the money underneath. 23 They took the things from inside the tent, brought them to Joshua and all the Israelites, and spread them out in the Lord's presence.

24 Then Joshua and all Israel with him took Achan son of Zerah, the silver, the cloak, and the bar of gold, his sons and daughters, his ox, donkey, and sheep, his tent, and all that he had, and brought them up to the Valley of Achor. 25 Joshua said, "Why have you troubled us? Today the Lord will trouble you!" So all Israel stoned him to death. They burned their bodies, threw stones on them, 26 and raised over him a large pile of rocks that remains to this day. Then the Lord turned from His burning anger. Therefore that place has been called the Valley of Achor to this day.

Joshua 7:1-26

PRINCIPLES TO LIVE BY

The story of Achan is a tale filled with grave warnings. We should examine our own hearts to see if we, like Achan, may be inclined to ignore God's commands and the welfare of His people in order to satisfy our own selfish desires. We should ask ourselves whether we, like Joshua and the army of Israel, have grown confident in ourselves and taken our eyes off of God, our true source of strength. Remember what Paul wrote the Corinthian believers, "Whoever thinks he stands must be careful not to fall!" (1 Cor. 10:12).

PRINCIPLE 1

GOD IS A HOLY GOD.

The Lord had revealed Himself to Israel on Mount Sinai as a holy God. The Law, the tabernacle, the ark of the covenant, and the elaborate sacrificial system all stressed to the Israelites that God was a holy God to be approached carefully and to be obeyed. When God declared that Jericho must be set apart to Him (Josh. 6:17), He expected Israel to regard that edict seriously. No Israelite soldier was to spare the life of anyone in Jericho or take any spoils from the battle site (vv. 18-19). Jericho was set apart to the holy God. Any breach of this command was an offense against His holiness.

PRINCIPLE 2

THE MORE LIGHT WE HAVE, THE MORE ACCOUNTABLE WE ARE.

A short time before Israel entered Canaan, Moses read the Law of God to the assembled people. Among his words were these: "The LORD your God will drive out these nations before you. ... You must burn up the carved images of their gods. Don't covet the silver or gold on the images and take it for yourself, or else you will be ensnared by it, for it is abhorrent to the LORD your God. You must not bring any abhorrent thing into your house, or you will be set apart for destruction like it. You are to utterly detest and abhor it, because it is set apart for destruction" (Deut. 7:22a, 25-26).

Achan disregarded God's explicit command. He lusted after some clothes and some money (Josh. 7:21). He should have regarded them with loathing as tainted by sin or with fear as the property of the holy God. Instead he took them and hid them so he could look good and live large when the conquest was completed. Achan put his creature comforts ahead of the commands of God. By doing so, he set himself apart to the same destruction intended for the things he took from Jericho (Deut. 7:26).

PRINCIPLE 3

BEWARE OF FLAGRANT LYING.

Achan lied by trying to hide his shameful deed once God revealed that the defeat at Ai stemmed from the disobedience of someone who had taken spoils from Jericho (Josh. 7:11). Maybe he thought others had taken more and would be punished instead. Perhaps he intended to look Joshua in the eye if he was accused and swear his innocence. He hadn't imagined that God would personally point him out by lot (vv. 16-19). He had put on his "game face" and hoped no one would ever figure it out. But lying was pointless with God hot on his trail.

In the New Testament Ananias and Sapphira sold property and pretended they had given the entire proceeds to meet the needs of the poor in the early church (Acts 5:1-11). The apostle Peter confronted this husband and wife individually about the truthfulness of their story. Each in turn lied and was struck dead by God. These stories correlate because each occurred at the start of a major work of God. Israel was entering the promised land and the church was in its infancy. Both Israel and the church have a foundational story concerning the inherent danger of trying to hide sin from God. We must not lie to Him.

PRINCIPLE 4

SEVERE JUDGMENT, ALTHOUGH UNLIKELY, COULD HAPPEN TODAY.

There have been times when God has severely judged Christians who flagrantly and deliberately destroyed unity in the church because of their own selfish and carnal motives (see 1 Cor. 3:16-17). Though this may not involve death, it nonetheless can be serious and painful judgment. When this has occurred, the sin has been so obvious that no one can misinterpret what has happened.

We must remind ourselves that even the Bible records few times when God broke through with this kind of judgment. When He did, it fell on people who had willfully disobeyed God in the full light of His revealed will and power. As in the instances of Achan as well as of Ananias and Sapphira, such judgment isn't primarily retribution against an especially evil individual. Rather, it provides protection or restores the well-being of the people of God.

EVERYBODY HAS SINNED!

Although Achan had flagrantly violated God's orders about setting apart the city of Jericho to Him, many others in Israel were guilty of other sins. Many of the fighting men came away from Jericho with feelings of pride and arrogance. The scouting party that initially surveyed Ai misjudged the military might of the town. They forgot that it was God who gave the victory at Jericho and assumed a small squad of their troops could skunk little Ai (Josh. 7:2-3).

Joshua and his commanders relied on their own strength at Ai. When their strength faltered, they all sank into despair and assumed God had let them down (vv. 5-7). Joshua had to deal with his own heart (v. 10) before God would use him to deal with Achan (vv. 11-12).

None of us dare point at the speck in someone else's eye before removing the log from his own eye (Matt. 7:1-5). Should God use us to confront someone about sin, we must do so humbly, with the full knowledge that we too are sinners (Gal. 6:1-2).

QUESTIONS FOR INTERACTION

1. When you first read Joshua 7, who did you identify with the most? Why that person?
   a. Achan
   b. Joshua
   c. The Israelite army
   d. The people of Ai
   e. Other _____

2. In what area of your life do you think you should apply the truth of this lesson?
   a. Your family relationships
   b. Your friendships
   c. Your work ethic
   d. Your personal finances
   e. A bad habit
   f. Other _____

3. Why is "burning" a good metaphor for anger? Why is it such a threatening word when applied to God's anger (Josh. 7:1, 26)?

LESSON 8

4. Why were Joshua and the army of Israel totally demoralized by only one defeat (vv. 4-9)?

5. How did God explain Israel's defeat at Ai (vv. 10-12)?

6. What do you suppose God wanted all the Israelites to be thinking about during the lengthy process of identifying the guilty party (vv. 13-15)?

7. What did God want Achan to think about and do while his tribe, clan, and family were being selected (vv. 16-18)?

8. Why was Achan not spared after he confessed his sin (vv. 19-23)?

9. Why did Achan receive the same fate as the things he stole (vv. 24-25)?

10. What did God teach Israel through this Achan incident that would stand them in good stead throughout the rest of their conquest of Canaan?

 ## GOING DEEPER

11. How does lying offend God's holy nature?

12. What are some of the subtle ways we are pressured to lie?

13. What are some sins today that threaten the unity and vitality of the body of Christ?

 ## CARING TIME

We need to be honest with one another when we see sin in a group member's life. We also need to be humble and gentle in confronting one another because we all fall into temptation. It's just a fact that men need other men to play the role of iron sharpening iron (Prov. 27:17). If Achan had had someone to confront him about his greedy desires for clothes and money, he might have avoided the calamity that destroyed him and his family.

1. Who do you count on to care about you enough to point out that your life is getting out of balance?

2. How does this group help keep your life on track so you don't offend God's holiness?

3. Let's close our Caring Time by praying around the group with each man praying for the integrity of the man to his right in the week ahead.

Next Week

Next week we'll look at the sequel to the story of Achan. Once the Israelite camp had been purged of the impurity of Achan's disobedience, Joshua planned a fresh assault on Ai. This time there would be no cockiness or arrogance. The whole army would attack, following a plan given Joshua by the Lord. This time the outcome would be very different.

Scripture Notes

Joshua 7:1-26

7:1-26 Out of an entire army of tens of thousands, surely Achan was not the only one who was tempted. Yet only he gave in to temptation and stole what was to be set apart to the Lord alone. As a result, their next battle at Ai was a total loss. It had to happen sooner or later, some might say. However, the tragedy of Achan's story was that sin, whenever it occurred, had to be punished.

7:2 Ai, ... near Beth-aven, west of Bethel. "Ai" means "The Ruins." It was probably the name by which this deserted site was known at the time the book of Joshua was written. The town likely had a different name before the battle that ruined it. Neither Ai nor Beth-aven has been definitively located by archaeologists, but Bethel has. These towns were about 10 miles west of Jericho atop the north-south ridge that forms the backbone of Palestine. Jericho lay below sea level; Ai some 3,000 feet above sea level. To capture little Ai was to command the high ground.

7:6 Joshua tore his clothes and fell. Picture the CEO of a major corporation solemnly tossing papers over his head during a frustrating board meeting. Imagine a football coach spiking his headset on the field. Joshua was in great distress at the news of this defeat. He could not imagine what had gone wrong. *Amorites.* "Amorite" meant something like "Westerner" or "mountain-dweller." Sometimes Amorite is used as a synonym for Canaanite, but not in this passage. The king of Ai probably was one of the Amorite kings who had been following Israel's exploits (5:1).

7:11 some of what was set apart. All living things were to be destroyed and burned in Jericho. Anything of value was to be brought into the Lord's treasury.

7:12 set apart for destruction. God had told Israel in the law that if they took things set apart for destruction, they themselves would be set apart for destruction (Deut. 7:26)

7:13 You will not be able to stand against your enemies. Israel's potential for victory was based upon obedience. According to God's wartime strategy, a perfectly obedient army of 10 could defeat tens of thousands of enemies. But one disobedient man amid tens of thousands of Israelites would bring defeat by even the weakest nation.

7:14 The tribe the LORD selects is to come forward. Achan woke up the next morning to a nightmare. In order to reveal the culprit, everyone had to assemble tribe by tribe, family by family, and individual by individual. In this type of supernatural lotto, no one wanted the winning number. Achan's ticket was already burning a hole underneath his tent.

7:21 200 silver shekels . . . gold weighing 50 shekels. Achan stole a little less than five pounds of silver and a little more than a pound of gold. Precious metals were not coined yet in the days of Joshua. They were weighed and value was assigned to units of weight.

7:24 Valley of Achor. Achor meant "disaster" or "trouble" in a devastating sense. The valley seems to have received its name at this time on the basis of this incident (v. 26).

7:25 They burned their bodies. This was supposed to be the original outcome of every living thing in Jericho (6:18-19, 24).

7:26 Then the LORD turned from His burning anger. Once the sin was removed from their midst, the Lord would once again walk with the Israelites.

PERSONAL NOTES ————————————————————

SECOND CHANCES WITH GOD

LAST WEEK

Last week we witnessed the sobering account of Israel's defeat at Ai. Flushed with confidence following the amazing conquest at Jericho and certain of easy victory, a small part of Israel's army trudged up the steep slopes to lofty Ai. They turned and fled back down in retreat and disarray. The Israelites did not yet realize that God had removed His presence and power because there was sin in the camp. One man had selfishly violated God's strict requirement that everyone and everything in Jericho be set apart to Him either for destruction as a sacrifice or placement in His treasury. God personally identified Achan by lot. Just as Joshua had clearly forewarned, Achan, his family, and his possessions were set apart to the fate the stolen objects should have received. God wants us to obey Him, to set ourselves apart holy because He is holy and because our personal actions affect the unity and vitality of His people (our family, church, community, and nation). After this sin was purged, Israel was ready for a fresh start—a second chance.

 ICEBREAKER

Second chances are wonderful things. Second chances at love. Second chances at happiness. Second chances at success. Second chances to right a wrong. Second chances often seem to be the stuff of stories rather than real life. Happily, God is a God of second chances. Mercy, grace, and forgiveness motivate our loving heavenly Father to redeem and regenerate sinners so we can be born again to live a new life or restored to useful service in His kingdom.

1. What is your favorite comeback story in fiction or real life?

2. Who do you know whose life has been blessed with a second chance at happiness? What was that person's second chance?

3. If you could choose a bad episode of your life for a second chance, what would it be?

LESSON 9

Once Joshua and the children of Israel carried out God's judgment on Achan, the obstacle to divine blessing on the nation disappeared. God moved immediately to reassure Joshua of His presence, renew this leader's courage, and get the conquest of Canaan back on track. Achan's sin did not mean God had forsaken His chosen people, nor did Joshua's immature response as a leader mean that God would not continue to use him as the chosen leader.

Some interesting differences emerge between how God directed Joshua at Jericho and how He led him at the second attack on Ai. God's attack plan for Jericho was detailed and lengthy. His directions concerning Ai were general and brief. Joshua had to fill in the details. God would not directly intervene during the battle. It would be a normal military operation. Ai's inhabitants were to be executed, but unlike Jericho the spoils of war would go to the conquering troops. How ironic and sad that Achan would have been given all that he needed and wanted … if he had waited on the Lord and not taken matters into his own hands.

God's Blessing Restored to Israel; Look Out Ai!

[1] The Lord said to Joshua, "Do not be afraid or discouraged. Take the whole military force with you and go attack Ai. Look, I have handed over to you the king of Ai, his people, city, and land. [2] Treat Ai and its king as you did Jericho and its king; you may plunder its spoil and livestock for yourselves. Set an ambush behind the city."

[3] So Joshua and the whole military force set out to attack Ai. Joshua selected 30,000 fighting men and sent them out at night. [4] He commanded them: "Pay attention. Lie in ambush behind the city, not too far from it, and all of you be ready. [5] Then I and all the people who are with me will approach the city. When they come out against us as they did the first time, we will flee from them. [6] They will come after us until we have drawn them away from the city, for they will say, 'They are fleeing from us as before.' While we are fleeing from them, [7] you are to come out of your ambush and seize the city, for the Lord your God has handed it over to you. [8] After taking the city, set it on fire. Follow the Lord's command—see [that you do] as I have ordered you." [9] So Joshua sent them out, and they went to the ambush site and waited between Bethel and Ai, to the west of Ai. But he spent that night with the troops.

[10] Joshua started early the next morning and mobilized them. Then he and the elders of Israel led the troops up to Ai. [11] All those who were

with him went up and approached the city, arriving opposite Ai, and camped to the north of it, with a valley between them and the city. [12] Now Joshua had taken about 5,000 men and set them in ambush between Bethel and Ai, to the west of the city. [13] The military force was stationed in this way: the main camp to the north of the city and its rear guard to the west of the city. And that night Joshua went into the valley.

[14] When the king of Ai saw [the Israelites] the men of the city hurried and went out early in the morning, so that he and all his people could engage Israel in battle at a suitable place facing the plain [of the Jordan]. But he did not know there was an ambush [waiting] for him behind the city. [15] Joshua and all Israel pretended to be beaten back by them and fled toward the wilderness. [16] Then all the troops of Ai were summoned to pursue them, and they pursued Joshua and were drawn away from the city. [17] Not a man was left in Ai or Bethel who did not go out after Israel, leaving the city exposed while they pursued Israel.

[18] Then the Lord said to Joshua, "Hold out the sword in your hand toward Ai, for I will hand the city over to you." So Joshua held out his sword toward it. [19] When he held out his hand, the men in ambush rose quickly from their position. They ran, entered the city, captured it, and immediately set it on fire.

[20] The men of Ai turned and looked back, and smoke from the city was rising to the sky! They could not escape in any direction, and the troops who had fled to the wilderness now became the pursuers. [21] When Joshua and all Israel saw that the [men in] ambush had captured the city and that smoke was rising from it, they turned back and struck down the men of Ai. [22] The men in the ambush came out of the city against them, and the men of Ai were [trapped] between the Israelite forces, some on one side and some on the other. They struck them down until no survivor or fugitive remained, [23] but they captured the king of Ai alive and brought him to Joshua.

[24] When Israel had finished killing everyone living in Ai who had pursued them into the open country, and when every last one of them had fallen by the sword, all Israel returned to Ai and struck it down with the sword. [25] The total of those who fell that day, both men and women, was 12,000—all the people of Ai. [26] Joshua did not draw back his hand that was holding the sword until all the inhabitants of Ai were completely destroyed. [27] Israel plundered only the cattle and spoil of that city for themselves, according to the Lord's command that He had given Joshua.

[28] Joshua burned Ai and left it a permanent ruin, desolate to this day. [29] He hung [the body of] the king of Ai on a tree until evening, and at sunset Joshua commanded that they take his body down from the tree.

They threw it down at the entrance of the city gate and put a large pile of rocks over it, which remains to this day.

Joshua 8:1-29

PRINCIPLES TO LIVE BY

The story of Achan is a cautionary tale about the dangers of disobedience. The story of the defeat of Ai is a comforting tale about God's ongoing commitment to blessing His people. He had not brought them out of Egypt, given them His law at Sinai, and shepherded them through 40 years of desert wandering to abandon them at Gilgal. Certainly He disciplined them sternly, but it was in order to ready them for greater victories.

PRINCIPLE 1

GOD WILL NEVER FORSAKE HIS CHILDREN, NO MATTER HOW MUCH THEY HAVE FORSAKEN HIM.

Achan had stolen a garment and a quantity of silver and gold from Jericho even though the Lord had set apart everyone and everything in the city for destruction. Joshua and his army reacted to the victory at Jericho with proud confidence. Their dependence on the Lord weakened. And when God disciplined Israel at Ai for Achan's sin, Joshua responded immaturely for such a seasoned leader.

However, the Lord had not forsaken Israel as Joshua and his army feared. Everything He did made it clear that He was challenging them to repent and return to Him with all their hearts. Today, God is displeased and disappointed when we too sin against Him and fail to do His will. However, no sin or failure can ever separate us from the love and care of God. He promised His true children eternal life based upon Christ's righteousness, not our own. He cannot lie and will not forsake us, no matter how much we fail Him.

The apostle Paul wrote the Romans: "For I am persuaded that neither death nor life, nor angels nor rulers, nor things present, nor things to come, nor powers, nor height, nor depth, nor any other created thing will have the power to separate us from the love of God that is in Christ Jesus our Lord!" (Rom. 8:38-39).

Just as God loves His children, He also disciplines them for their benefit to develop holiness and Christ-like character. Although discipline is painful, "later on it yields the fruit of peace and righteousness to those that have trained by it" (Heb. 12: 11). God wants us to learn from the discipline and turn once again to Him to walk in His will and in the light of His unconditional love (1 John 1:5-9).

PRINCIPLE 2

GOD CAN TAKE THE MISTAKES HIS CHILDREN MAKE AND TURN THEM INTO POSITIVE RESULTS.

When Israel finally defeated Ai, Joshua wisely based his strategy on their original battle plan and subsequent defeat. When the army of Ai burst from its city gates, the army of Israel turned and ran away as it had before. The army of Ai pursued Israel without hesitation. It never occurred to them that anything was different this time around.

But things were different. The army of Israel was back under the control and blessing of God. God used the earlier setback to position Israel's enemy for total destruction. Only God is able to weave the calamities of life into a tapestry of victory. Again Paul wrote the Romans: "We know that all things work together for the good of those who love God: those who are called according to His purpose" (Rom. 8:28).

Often, God works through our sins and mistakes to call us back to a renewed commitment to obedience and relationship with Him. We'll see an example of this next week in Joshua 8:30-35.

PRINCIPLE 3

GOD NORMALLY GIVES US FREEDOM TO DEVELOP A STRATEGIC PLAN BUT IT MUST ALWAYS BE IN HARMONY WITH HIS BASIC GUIDELINES AND PRINCIPLES.

God gave Joshua a basic plan for attacking Ai. "Take the whole military force with you and go attack Ai. ... Set an ambush behind the city" (Josh. 8:1b, 2b). Evidently the Lord did not fill in the details. He gave Joshua freedom to devise additional plans that were in harmony with His general plan. On his part, Joshua stayed constantly alert to God's guidance as he developed and worked out his plan.

Today God gives us clear guidelines and principles in His Word for carrying out His will in this world. When we work within these parameters, we have unusual freedom to develop unique strategies that He may bless. We must not, however, take matters into our own hands and neglect His revealed will for our lives.

Questions for Interaction

1. How does daring to take risks lead to getting second chances in life?

2. How does trusting God lead to getting second chances in life?

3. What was the broad outline of God's plan for capturing Ai (Josh. 8:1-2)?

4. What details did Joshua add to flesh out God's general plan (vv. 5-8, 12-13)?

5. Joshua stationed two forces west of Ai (vv. 3-4, 12). The larger group was to seize the deserted city; the smaller group may have been a rear guard against any force from Bethel. What strategy emptied Ai so the troops in ambush could attack it (vv. 14-17)?

6. How did the army of Israel defeat the army of Ai (vv. 18-23)?

7. What was the fate of Ai, its inhabitants, and its king (vv. 24-29)?

8. How many piles of stone had Joshua and Israel erected in Canaan so far, and what did each of them mark?

9. How did Joshua use the earlier defeat by the army of Ai against Ai when he attacked the second time?

10. If Achan had trusted God and controlled his greed at Jericho, how would he have felt after the defeat of Ai?

Going Deeper

11. What are some areas of life in which men often need second chances?

12. How can the church be used of God to encourage people who need a fresh start in some area of life?

13. What role does suffering and the discipline of God play in preparing a person to appreciate and benefit from a "second chance"?

CARING TIME

Most of us struggle with persistent attitudes or habits we would like to be rid of. After a lesson about second chances, it might be a good time to share some of these with the group so we can pray for one another and hold one another accountable for dealing with them.

1. What attitude or habit that you struggle with regularly would you like a "second chance" in overcoming?

2. How have you tried to overcome this attitude or habit in the past?

3. Let's take turns praying in the group, with each of you praying for one other man here.

NEXT WEEK

Next week we examine a renewal of the covenant between the Lord and Israel. Joshua had led the army of Israel out of the Jordan valley into the high country of central Canaan at Ai. The promised land had been effectively invaded and divided. Before launching successive campaigns south and north, Joshua led Israel to twin mountain peaks for a formal ceremony that would ground that generation in commitment to the law of God.

SCRIPTURE NOTES

JOSHUA 8:1-29

8:1 Joshua, "Do not be afraid." God addressed Joshua's initial fears of returning to a city where Israel had just been defeated.

8:1-29 Look, I have handed over to you. Same city. Different battle. Different outcome. Now, with the Lord's presence and power, the Israelites destroyed the city of Ai.

8:2 you may plunder its spoil and livestock. This time, the soldiers were entitled to the riches of their victory. If only Achan had waited.

8:13 stationed in this way. The strategy here was to catch the people of Ai in their over-confidence. With an ambush set for the city, and a plan to lure the fighting men away, Israel's victory was certain. Romans 8:31b says it all: "If God is for us, who is against us?"

8:17 Bethel. A secondary unit of 5,000 troops was strategically placed between Bethel and Ai in order to cut off possible reinforcements.

8:26 all . . . were completely destroyed. Two battles. Two leveled cities. It was important that the army of Israel become known for complete victory in its initial battles.

8:29 a large pie of rocks. Like bookmarks in Israel's history, these memorials began popping up across the landscape of Canaan. Although grisly at points, each one symbolized God's might in its own way.

PERSONAL NOTES

LESSON 9

BACK TO BASICS

LAST WEEK

Last week we studied how Israel bounced back from the defeat caused by Achan's sin, and went on to conquer the city of Ai. Perched atop the ridge of the central highlands of Canaan, Ai and its neighbors controlled the high ground. By seizing that territory, Joshua and Israel broke the back of any united Canaanite opposition and set the stage for strategic campaigns south and north to conquer the promised land. At the time of the battle of Ai, however, no one was looking ahead. They were all tremendously relieved to bask once again in the protection and blessing of God. We mentioned last week that often, God works through our sins and mistakes to call us back to a renewed commitment to obedience and relationship with Him. Israel needed that return to the basics and Joshua knew it.

ICEBREAKER

If you're an athlete, you might "get back to basics" for many reasons. Maybe you're in a slump and want to re-orient yourself to fundamental skills. Maybe you've achieved your recent goals and want to take your game to the next level. Maybe you're coming off an injury and need to get back in shape. Maybe you've got a new coach who wants to alter the way you play the game. Improvement, change, conditioning—share the common strategic element of the vital need of getting back to the basics, the fundamentals. Every good coach knows that practicing the fundamentals often makes the difference between winning and losing.

1. When you play a new game, how do you like to learn the rules?
    a. Read the rules carefully.
    b. Have someone explain the rules to you.
    c. Play a practice game and learn the rules as you play.
    d. Make them up as you go.
    e. Rules, we have rules?
    f. Other _____.

2. In your occupation, what are "the basics" a person needs to master?

3. Where have you carved your initials, written you name, or left some other mark to indicate that you were there?

Once the Israelite army secured a foothold in the highlands of Canaan, the road north to Shechem was open. Shechem lay in a valley between two mountains, Ebal to the north and Gerizim to the south. Both mountains figured in the next episode of the book of Joshua. Before the children of Israel ever entered the promised land, Moses told them specifically to build a stone monument to the Law and an altar for sacrifices to the Lord at Mount Ebal (Deut. 27:4-7).

Getting Back in the Groove

[30] At that time Joshua built an altar on Mount Ebal to the Lord, the God of Israel, [31] just as Moses the Lord's servant had commanded the Israelites. He built it according to what is written in the book of the law of Moses: an altar of uncut stones on which no iron tool has been used. Then they offered burnt offerings to the Lord and sacrificed fellowship offerings on it. [32] There on the stones, Joshua copied the law of Moses, which he had written in the presence of the Israelites. [33] All Israel, foreigner and citizen alike, with their elders, officers, and judges, stood on either side of the ark of the Lord's covenant facing the Levitical priests who carried it. As Moses the Lord's servant had commanded earlier, half of them were in front of Mount Gerizim and half in front of Mount Ebal, to bless the people of Israel. [34] Afterwards, Joshua read aloud all the words of the law—the blessings as well as the curses— according to all that is written in the book of the law. [35] There was not a word of all that Moses had commanded that Joshua did not read before the entire assembly of Israel, including the women, little children, and foreigners who were with them.

Joshua 8:30-35

The Law of God was foundational to the life of Israel. At the covenant renewal ceremony at mounts Ebal and Gerizim, Israel for the third time formally vowed to obey God. No matter how many direct revelations of His will the Lord made to Joshua, His Word contained in His law was still the most basic communication to mankind. Nothing replaces the eternal, written Word of God in His dealings with humanity. That is even more true today than it was in the days of Joshua since we now have God's completed revelation in the Bible.

LESSON 10

PRINCIPLE 1

WE MUST TAKE TIME ON A CONSISTENT BASIS TO MAINTAIN AND, WHEN NEEDED, REGAIN PERSPECTIVE ON GOD'S WILL FOR OUR LIVES.

In the middle of Joshua 8, the narrative shifts suddenly from "a large pile of rocks" at the gates of Ai (v. 29) to "an altar on Mount Ebal" (v. 30). Both are stacked stone structures. One symbolized the defeat of Ai; the other symbolized worship of the Lord. One looked forward and focused on the task at hand; the other looked back and focused on the God in whose service Israel was pursuing this task.

Joshua was functioning like a good coach taking his team back to basics. In this case, the basics involved reviewing and applying God's covenant, which He had made with Israel at Mount Sinai. The people needed this reminder so that no one else would lose focus as Achan had done at Jericho. Joshua himself needed this reminder so he would not lose heart as he had done when Israel lost its initial skirmish at Ai.

Like Israel, we need to engage in two processes to keep our perspective on God's will. *First, we need to review the teachings of Scripture regularly* (Josh. 1:8 and other passages suggest day and night). God's Word is the only reliable and absolute source for information about God's will for us. When we get too busy for the Bible, we will lose perspective on God's direction for our lives. *Second, we need to maintain our relationship with God.* This relationship depends on personal meditation and prayer, as well as on corporate worship and prayer.

When we're alone with God, we can meditate on His Word and wait for the promptings of His Spirit. But we must not forget relationships with other believers in helping us determine and do God's will. It's virtually impossible to develop a warm, meaningful relationship with the Lord if we are not developing warm, meaningful relationships with other members of the body of Christ. Hebrews 10:19-25 exhorts us to draw near to the "sanctuary"—the very presence of God. But this same passage also exhorts us to "be concerned about one another in order to promote love and good works, not staying away from our meetings, as some habitually do, but encouraging each other, and all the more as [we] see the day drawing near."

PRINCIPLE 2

GOD NEVER PROMISED HE WOULD DIRECTLY REVEAL HIS SPECIFIC WILL TO US EVERY TIME WE NEED TO MAKE A DECISION.

Joshua led Israel at a time when the first five books of the Old Testament were the entirety of the Scripture that was in writing. God spoke to him and gave him specific guidance quite often. Even so, Joshua knew that the written law of God was the general framework that made sense of life, including the individual acts of divine guidance he received.

God had given His law at Mount Sinai (Ex. 34). Forty years later, Moses had read the law to Israel in a covenant renewal ceremony on the plains of Moab east of Jordan shortly before his death (Deut. 5). Now, some months later, all of Israel "including the women, little children, and foreigners who were with them" would listen to the law again (Josh. 8:35). For Joshua and Israel, success and prosperity depended on knowing, meditating on, and obeying this law (Josh. 1:8).

Today we need to commit ourselves to becoming thoroughly familiar with and committed to the Word of God, which we possess in its completed form. Divine revelation forms the framework within which we can make proper decisions about the details of life. Too many Christians ignore their responsibility to know and apply the concepts and commands He has already revealed in the Bible.

Keep in mind these five considerations as you determine God's will in any particular situation.

(1) Is there any statement in God's written revelation that supports or is in opposition to the direction you are inclined to go? Don't expect, for instance, God's approval of marriage to an unbeliever or divorce based solely on incompatibility. If our feelings, the advice we're getting, or our impressions of the "Holy Spirit's prompting," don't conform to Scripture, then we should not move in those directions.

(2) What do other mature Christians, including your pastor, church elders, and parents, think about a course of action? What advice do they give? Corporate wisdom from godly people is significant in God's scheme of things (Eph. 4:16). This is another reason not to stay away from our meetings with other Christians (Heb. 10:25). The wisdom of mature counselors makes a good supplement to our knowledge of the Bible.

(3) What has the Spirit of God revealed to you? God reveals and clarifies truth to us by His Spirit, who "searches everything, even the deep things of God" (See 1 Cor. 2:10-16). However, we are warned to be careful to "test the spirits to determine if they are from God" (1 John 4:1-3).

(4) What circumstances suggest this may be a right or wrong decision? The Bible commands. Wise counselors advise. Circumstances can only suggest. A course of action may fit really well into the pattern of your life. It may not.

(5) How do I feel about a possible course of action? Consult your feelings last. Don't feel guilty about something you really want to do, if it passes the first three tests. On the other hand, keep in mind that every major decision will kick up anxiety and create stress. You may often be

afraid to do the very things you should. In those cases, be careful not to equate feelings of fear with what may appear to be the Holy Spirit's promptings.

QUESTIONS FOR INTERACTION

1. How would you rate your knowledge of the Bible?
   a. I've studied the Bible regularly since I was a boy and know it well.
   b. I've studied the Bible as an adult and know quite a bit.
   c. I read the Bible regularly and have a good grasp of the basics.
   d. I don't read the Bible a lot, but I've learned some from listening to preaching.
   e. I don't know an epistle from an apostle.
   f. Other _____.

2. When do you wish you knew the Bible better?
   a. When I don't know the answers to questions about the Bible
   b. When I face temptation
   c. When I need to make a major decision about the direction of my life
   d. When I want to talk to a friend about Christ
   e. When I don't know what to do as a husband or father
   f. Other _____

3. How did Joshua build the altar on Mount Ebal (Josh. 8:30-31)?

4. Why did Joshua build this altar (v. 31)?

5. Why did Joshua set up large stones coated with plaster (v. 32; see Deut. 27:2, 8)?

6. Where did the people stand and where were the priests with the ark during the covenant ceremony (v. 33)?

7. Why do you think Joshua was careful to read every word of Moses to every man, woman, and child associated with Israel (vv. 34-35)?

8. Why were foreigners choosing to associate with Israel (v. 35)?

9. What should mounts Ebal and Gerizim have meant to future generations of Israelites?

10. Recount a time when you realized as never before that the Bible contained essential information for your life.

Going Deeper

11. How can you use the Bible to gain perspective on God's will for your life?

12. When you have a major decision to make, what insight do you want from God's Word to help make it?

13. How do you balance searching the Scriptures with the revelation of the Holy Spirit, the wisdom of godly counselors, circumstances, and emotions in determining God's specific direction and guidance in your life?

14. Joshua 1:8 reads, "This book of instruction must not depart from your mouth; you are to recite it day and night, so that you may carefully observe everything written in it. For then you will prosper and succeed in whatever you do." What do you suppose happens to people who neglect to read, study, and obey God's Word?

Caring Time

We have the opportunity to help one another make good decisions. In Principle 2, we're reminded that what other mature Christians think about a matter can give us wisdom to supplement our insight from the Bible. We can also help one another evaluate our circumstances and our feelings as they come into play in decision making.

1. What decisions are you currently struggling with?

2. What insights would others in our group have about these situations?

3. Let's close with prayer for each of these pending decisions, asking God for extreme clarity from His Word, aligned with confirmation by His Spirit, godly counsel, circumstances, and our emotions.

Next Week

Next week we will learn that Joshua and Israel were susceptible to deception, even though they had just renewed their covenant with God. Some local Canaanites disguised themselves to look as people who had come a long distance and they tricked Joshua into forming a mutual defense pact with them. They flattered Israel and lied about where they were from. No one checked their story, and suddenly a town in Canaan was safe from attack. Satan is a subtle liar. We have to be on guard against his scheming.

Scripture Notes

Joshua 8:30-35

8:30-35 Usually a victorious army either celebrates or strategizes its next move. Joshua did both, but neither in the traditional sense. His celebration involved an altar of sacrifice and his strategy was to stop and review the laws of Moses.

8:30 an altar on Mount Ebal. Joshua led them here along 30 miles of uninhabited land so they could prepare for a spiritual event without having to look over their shoulders for potential attackers.

8:31 as Moses ... had commanded. Moses had spelled out the location and details of this covenant renewal ceremony before he died on the other side of the Jordan. The details of the ceremony are in Deuteronomy 27–28. *uncut stones.* In Exodus 20:24-25, the law directed that altars erected for special occasions should be made of earth or uncut stones. The stones would "be defiled" if changed by human tools from the shape God gave them in nature.

8:32 on the stones, Joshua copied the law of Moses. These were not the same stones the altar was made of. No one knows for sure how much of Moses' law was meticulously copied onto these large stones coated with plaster (Deut. 27:2, 8). Inscribing the Ten Commandments alone would have been quite a feat. Yet, this could refer to as much as the entire law in Deuteronomy.

8:33 All Israel. Imagine having a family meeting with over two million participants! *foreigner and citizen alike.* Many non-Hebrews had attached themselves to Israel. "An ethnically diverse crowd" left Egypt with Israel (Ex. 12:38). Perhaps others from surrounding nations had joined during the wilderness wandering. Some, if not all of these, invaded Canaan with Israel. Certainly Rahab and her family were among the "foreigners." *half ... in front of Mount Gerizim and half in front of Mount Ebal.* The two congregations of Israel faced one another across the valley between the mountains (Deut. 27:12-13). The Gerizim tribes called out "Amen" when the Levites read the blessings that would accompany covenant obedience (Deut. 27:14-26). The Ebal tribes called out "Amen" when the curses were read that would accompany covenant disobedience (Deut. 28:3-6).

PERSONAL NOTES ———————————————

EXCEPTIONAL DECEPTION

LAST WEEK

Last week we joined Joshua and the children of Israel obeying one
of Moses' last commands by holding a covenant renewal ceremony in the
promised land. Joshua led the people to Mount Ebal and Mount Gerizim
where he built an altar for sacrifices and erected a monument with the
words of the law. The Levites led the people in affirming the blessings that
would be theirs for keeping the covenant as well as the curses they could
expect if they broke it. The people renewed their commitment to the
fundamentals of their faith that would sustain them through the coming
wars. Despite this renewed commitment and refocusing, the world was
still full of trouble, and deception lurked at Joshua's door.

ICEBREAKER

Deception is a strange phenomenon. It creates suspense in stories. It
makes surprise parties fun. It puts the "kick" into harmless pranks. On the
other hand, deception destroys friendships and marriages. It cheats people
out of their money and their homes. It can weaken the entire fabric of a
society.

1. What's the best April Fool's trick you've ever pulled on anyone or had
   someone pull on you?

2. Think about movies or books with surprise endings. Which one had
   the best surprise ending that you never saw coming?

3. When was the worst time that you've been deceived by a salesperson?
   How did that make you feel?

BIBLICAL FOUNDATION

Joshua had faced the defeat at Ai with unusual courage. As difficult
as it had been, he dealt with Achan's sin. Furthermore, he built an altar to
the Lord and "offered burnt offerings" and "sacrificed fellowship offerings"
to the Lord on Mount Ebal (Josh. 8:31). All Israel had acknowledged God

and worshiped Him as their protector and provider. Everything seemed to be in order for Joshua and Israel to move forward victoriously. Then a town just down the road from Ai played a cunning trick on Joshua that no one saw coming. Too bad Joshua and his leaders did not consult the Lord and got caught with their prayers down!

Caught Off Guard

³ When the inhabitants of Gibeon heard what Joshua had done to Jericho and Ai, ⁴ they acted deceptively. They gathered provisions and took worn-out sacks on their donkeys and old wineskins, cracked and mended. ⁵ [They wore] old, patched sandals on their feet and threadbare clothing on their bodies. Their entire provision of bread was dry and crumbly. ⁶ They went to Joshua in the camp at Gilgal and said to him and the men of Israel, "We have come from a distant land. Please make a treaty with us."

⁷ The men of Israel replied to the Hivites, "Perhaps you live among us. How can we make a treaty with you?"

⁸ They said to Joshua, "We are your servants."

Then Joshua asked them, "Who are you and where do you come from?"

⁹ They replied to him, "Your servants have come from a far away land because of the reputation of the Lord your God. For we have heard of His fame, and all that He did in Egypt, ¹⁰ and all that He did to the two Amorite kings beyond the Jordan—Sihon king of Heshbon and Og king of Bashan, who was in Ashtaroth. ¹¹ So our elders and all the inhabitants of our land told us, 'Take provisions with you for the journey; go and meet them and say, "We are your servants. Please make a treaty with us."' ¹² This bread of ours was warm when we took it from our houses as food on the day we left to come to you. But take a look, it is now dry and crumbly. ¹³ These wineskins were new when we filled them, but look, they are cracked. And these clothes and sandals of ours are worn out from the extremely long journey." ¹⁴ Then the men [of Israel] took some of their provisions, but did not seek the Lord's counsel. ¹⁵ So Joshua established peace with them and made a treaty to let them live, and the leaders of the community swore an oath to them.

¹⁶ Three days after making the treaty with them, they heard that the Gibeonites were their neighbors, living among them. ¹⁷ So the Israelites set out and reached the Gibeonite cities on the third day. Now their cities were Gibeon, Chephirah, Beeroth, and Kiriath-jearim. ¹⁸ But the Israelites did not attack them, because the leaders of the community had

sworn an oath to them by the Lord, the God of Israel. Then the whole community grumbled against the leaders.

[19] All the leaders answered them, "We have sworn an oath to them by the Lord, the God of Israel, and now we cannot touch them. [20] This is how we will treat them: we will let them live, so that no wrath will fall on us because of the oath we swore to them." [21] They also said, "Let them live." So the Gibeonites became woodcutters and water carriers for the whole community, as the leaders had promised them.

[22] Joshua summoned the Gibeonites and said to them, "Why did you deceive us by telling us you live far away from us, when in fact you live among us? [23] Therefore you are cursed and will always be slaves—woodcutters and water carriers for the house of my God."

[24] The Gibeonites answered him, "It was clearly reported to your servants that the Lord your God had commanded His servant Moses to give you all the land and to destroy all the inhabitants of the land before you. We greatly feared for our lives because of you, and that is why we did this. [25] Now we are in your hands. Do to us whatever you think is right." [26] This is what Joshua did to them: he delivered them from the hands of the Israelites, and they did not kill them. [27] On that day he made them woodcutters and water carriers—as they are today—for the community and for the Lord's altar at the place He would choose.

Joshua 9:3-27

PRINCIPLES TO LIVE BY

Joshua made a treaty with the Gibeonites based on persuasive evidence. He acted as he thought God wanted him to in such cases. However, the "persuasive evidence" was all fraud. If Joshua had been more cautious, asked probing questions, and taken more time to reach a decision, he might have uncovered the Gibeonites' deception. More significantly, Joshua made this decision without seeking "the LORD's counsel" (Josh. 9:14). Without God's input, Joshua misinterpreted circumstances, misapplied Scripture, and ended up looking like he'd been caught with his pants down. Joshua's misstep should caution us all to handle God's Word more carefully and seek His wisdom so we can find dependable guidance and keen spiritual discernment. Some errors, like Joshua's, are irreversible, but never without hope.

CHRISTIANS CAN BE LED ASTRAY BY MAKING SUPERFICIAL
JUDGMENTS WITHOUT ACCURATELY DIVIDING GOD'S WORD OF TRUTH.

Perhaps some of the people of Gibeon had been "listening in" when Joshua reviewed the law of God at Mount Ebal and Mount Gerizim. In some way they knew that Israel was forbidden to make treaties with people in the land of Canaan (Ex. 23:31-33) but not with those from outside the land (Deut. 20:10-12). The Gibeonites broke ranks with the other Canaanite cities that intended to wage war together against Israel (Josh. 9:1-2). They convinced Joshua they were from a far country and made a mutual-defense treaty with Israel.

Satan comes to us in the same way. He is a subtle enemy, and lying is one of his common tactics. He takes special delight in twisting God's very words to achieve his insidious goals. He tempted Jesus by quoting Psalm 91:11-12 out of context (Matt. 4:6). He tries to get us to misunderstand and misapply the Bible too. It's very important to learn how to study and apply God's Word accurately. We also need to listen critically to those who teach us the Bible to be sure they are interpreting it correctly.

PRINCIPLE 2

WE CAN BE DECEIVED IF WE MISUSE THE BIBLE AS AN
ENCHANTED CRYSTAL BALL.

The Bible is meant to be read and understood according to standard grammatical and historical methods of interpreting literature. We reviewed in our last lesson that the Holy Spirit helps us comprehend and apply the inspired Word of God. Though God can enlighten each of us through personal study, it's much safer to seek His will within a community of faith. Together as believers, we can develop the "mind of Christ" to discern spiritual significance, to evaluate spiritual truth within the bounds of Scripture, and to receive the spiritual power of God's Word. (2 Cor. 2:15). If we do not become students of God's Word, we can easily fall prey to using the Bible as a superficial, instant answer tool.

Unfortunately, many Christians want to treat the Bible mystically, if not magically. With this approach, a reader takes the words of a passage with little or no attention to its context and looks for some special, personal meaning for his life that day. Such a person might read Joshua 9 and conclude God is telling him someone will try to trick him into making a bad deal at work that day. Such a Bible student wants immediate guidance from the Bible of the sort promised by crystal balls, horoscopes, and fortune cookies.

LESSON 11

PRINCIPLE 3

WE CAN BE DECEIVED IF WE READ OR STUDY THE BIBLE
SUBJECTIVELY WITHOUT GOOD PRINCIPLES OF INTERPRETATION.

We should never make the mistake of coming to the Scriptures
to substantiate or prove our predetermined ideas. The Bible can be
made to say almost anything if we ignore the basic principles of literary
interpretation. Some people come to the Bible expecting to interact
with the history and meaning of the biblical texts, but don't know how.
Sometimes we are overwhelmed by Old Testament books of history or
prophecy that seem impossible to understand. Worse yet, we may read
the teachings of Jesus in the Gospels and find His statements extreme or
obscure. It can be discouraging to find the words of our own Lord difficult
to grasp.

Use the following three guidelines to avoid bad interpretation. (1)
Determine what words, phrases, and sentences mean in the context of the
passage or book. Use a Bible dictionary, concordance, or commentary.
(2) Investigate the historical and cultural background setting of a Bible
passage. Commentaries, atlases, and Bible background books can help
you understand the setting and the original meaning. (3) Adopt a literal
meaning for a passage unless there are literary reasons to do otherwise.
There are lots of poems, parables, and figures of speech in the Bible
that need to be understood figuratively. That doesn't mean you look for
unusual meanings in ordinary prose.

PRINCIPLE 4

WE CAN BE DECEIVED IF WE BRING CIRCUMSTANCES TO BEAR ON
SCRIPTURE RATHER THAN EVALUATING CIRCUMSTANCES IN LIGHT OF
SCRIPTURE.

Circumstances deceived Joshua. He made a treaty with the Gibeonites
because surface evidence indicated they were a nation that lived far away.
Everything looked right to Joshua, but circumstances were not as they
appeared.

We all tend to evaluate events in the light of our circumstances. Satan
takes pleasure in getting us to misunderstand the Bible in the light of our
natural tendencies, cultural preferences, and psychological makeup.

Fortunately, most of our mistakes are reversible. Even in Joshua's
case, he did what he could to correct the situation without committing a
second sin by trying to undo the first one. In Christ, there's always hope,
no matter what our past mistakes.

QUESTIONS FOR INTERACTION

1. In what area of your life do you wish you had more discernment so you could make the hard calls without messing up?

2. When you do make mistakes, which of these best describes how you handle them? Be honest with yourself.
   a. I try to put the best spin on them to save face.
   b. I apologize profusely and promise to do better.
   c. I get depressed and want to escape.
   d. I accept responsibility and assess how to prevent a reoccurrence.
   e. I deny my role or pass the blame to others.
   f. Other _____.

3. How did the Gibeonites deceive Joshua and the other leaders of Israel (Josh. 9:3-6, 9-13)?

4. What were the motives of the Gibeonites (vv. 3, 24-25)? What was the worst part of their motivation? What was the best?

5. Why didn't Joshua revoke the treaty since it was based on lies (vv. 15, 18)? What do you think of that reasoning?

6. What was the final fate of the Gibeonites (vv. 15, 19-21, 23, 26-27)?

7. How satisfied do you suppose the Gibeonites were with the final outcome of their scheme? Why?

8. How could Joshua have avoided the mess-up with the Gibeonites?

9. From what sources can you find the wisdom and counsel you need to become more discerning in the area you identified in question 1?

GOING DEEPER

10. How would you complete this sentence: "To become a better Bible student, I need to …"?
    a. Start learning the ABCs of Bible study.
       (Some good resources are *How to Study the Bible for Yourself* by Tim LaHaye and *Disciplines of a Godly Man* by Kent Hughes along with helpful online resources available at www.biblestudytools.net, www.bible.gospelcom.net/tools, and www.bible.lifeway.com)

b. Use the training and skills I already have.

c. Learn more about Bible study than I already know.

d. Surround my Bible study times with prayer, inviting the Holy Spirit to direct my mind and heart.

e. Other _____.

11. When have you seen someone take a biblical truth and use it incorrectly?

12. When have you been tempted by Satan or your own worldly desires to use a biblical truth selfishly or manipulatively? How can you become wise to this tactic of your enemy, the devil?

 CARING TIME

This lesson could become oppressive if we conclude that we're in danger of falling into some fiendish trap every time we make an obvious decision. That isn't so. The devil and his agents are real, and they want to destroy us. However, God's heavenly forces and the Holy Spirit are just as real. God is more powerful than the forces of evil, and He is committed to protecting and strengthening us. He has promised that if we put on the whole armor of God, we can defeat Satan (Eph. 6:10-18).

The spirit realm is real, but we aren't to spend our days brooding about what we can't see. God has given us His Word to guide our lives. The Bible tells us how to treat people and situations in our everyday world and how to rely on Him concerning all that occurs in the unseen realm around us. That's why we're emphasizing how to handle God's Word correctly.

1. What have you learned about reading and understanding the Bible during the time you've been in this group?

2. How about the importance of seeking God in prayer?

3. What books, courses, or other resources have helped you learn how to study the Bible?

4. What could we do in this group to help you with your goals in question 10 above?

NEXT WEEK

Next week we'll jump ahead in the book of Joshua to an event near the end of the conquest of Canaan. We'll marvel at how an 85-year-old man named Caleb bravely claimed his family's inheritance within the tribal territory of Judah. Forty-five years earlier, Caleb and Joshua had been among the 12 spies sent out by Moses to scout the promised land. They were the only two who came back to Kadesh-barnea excited about invading Canaan. Forty years of wandering resulted from the cowardice of the other spies and the people of Israel. God promised Caleb he would some day personally receive a family inheritance in Canaan. After 45 years, God kept His promise, and Caleb claimed his land. Caleb stayed faithful all those years because he trusted in the character and promises of God.

SCRIPTURE NOTES

JOSHUA 9:3-27

9:3-27 the people of Gibeon. This section records how the fame of the children of Israel actually served to work against them in some respects. The Gibeonites, aware of the Israelites' recent victories and mildly familiar with the law of Moses, used this information for their own good. According to the law, Israel was allowed to make treaties with people outside the land (Ex. 23:31-33; 34:12). However, it was to utterly destroy nearby cities. Neighbors with Ai, the city of Gibeon knew it had to come up with a plan.

9:3 inhabitants of Gibeon. Not willing to remain a sitting duck, the city of Gibeon sought to protect its strategic positioning in Canaan.

9:4 they acted deceptively. What they may have lacked in courage, they made up for in cunning.

9:6 come from a distant land ... make a treaty with us. The Gibeonites hoped to avoid both the truth and its consequences. The truth about their actual homeland would have brought consequences they could not bear—certain destruction. So they lied to gain a treaty that would save their lives.
9:7 Hivites. The Hivites (HIGH-vites) were one of the Canaanite tribes (Gen. 10:17) that Israel was instructed to destroy (Ex. 13:5; 23:23). The Gibeonites were a part of that tribe.

9:14 men of Israel ... did not seek the LORD's counsel. Although it may have seemed an obvious move, the officers who inspected the claims of the Gibeonites did so only on the basis of their own insight. They did not seek God's direction, which might have exposed the Gibeonites' game.

9:18 the whole community grumbled against the leaders. The whole community may have professed their suspicions after the jig was up, but it was too late at that point. A vow had already been made and the honorable thing for Israel to do was to uphold that vow—even though it was obtained dishonestly.

PERSONAL NOTES

A Strong Finish

Last Week

Last week we studied the surprising incident in which the residents of nearby Gibeon cooked up an elaborate scheme to convince Joshua that they lived a long way away. Through this deception, they convinced Joshua to make a mutual-defense treaty with them as allowed by the law of Moses (Deut. 20:10-12). When Joshua found out they were local Canaanites, he could do nothing to them because of the treaty. We concluded that we, as men and leaders, need to be cautious about interpreting the circumstances of life. We need to be careful students of God's Word and men of prayer so we have the very best divine perspective on all that's going on around us.

Icebreaker

This lesson turns the spotlight on a guy named Caleb. Once Caleb had been an important guy, but he had faded into the background. A generation had grown up who didn't know about his glory years. Then one day Caleb stepped forward to announce that God had promised him something special 45 years ago and it was time to collect on that promise. Joshua remembered, and whole-heartedly supported this.

1. What do you expect to inherit some day?
   a. Real estate
   b. Money
   c. A business
   d. Bad debts and a mess to take care of
   e. Some objects of sentimental value
   f. Other _____

2. When you were a boy, was there a particular object or prize that you set your sights on to possess or win? What did you do to pursue it? Did you get it? How did that make you feel?

3. Describe a time you felt sorry for yourself because you were passed over, serving thanklessly in the background while someone else stole the limelight.

Israel spent about seven years conquering the 31 Canaanite kings (Josh. 12:1-24). At the end of that time, the Lord directed Joshua to divide the promised land among the tribes of Israel. However, pockets of Canaanite resistance remained in every region, and once the tribes received their inheritance, they were responsible to complete the task of conquest (Josh. 13:1-7).

The tribe of Judah expressed the most eagerness to take hold of their allotted territory (Josh. 14:6). These people exemplified the attitude God wanted all the tribes to have toward possessing and securing their land. Within Judah, one 85-year-old man named Caleb stood head and shoulders above all others in determination to seize the moment to serve the Lord and secure his inheritance.

When the Going Gets Tough, the Tough Get Going!

⁶ The descendants of Judah approached Joshua at Gilgal, and Caleb son of Jephunneh the Kenizzite said to him, "You know what the Lord promised Moses the man of God at Kadesh-barnea about you and me. ⁷ I was 40 years old when Moses the Lord's servant sent me from Kadesh-barnea to scout the land, and I brought back an honest report. ⁸ My brothers who went with me caused the people's hearts to melt with fear, but I remained loyal to the Lord my God. ⁹ On that day Moses promised me, 'The land where you have set foot will be an inheritance for you and your descendants forever, because you have remained loyal to the Lord my God.

¹⁰ "As you see, the Lord has kept me alive [these] 45 years as He promised, since the Lord spoke this word to Moses while Israel was journeying in the wilderness. Here I am today, 85 years old. ¹¹ I am still as strong today as I was the day Moses sent me out. My strength for battle and for daily tasks is now as it was then. ¹² Now give me this hill country the Lord promised [me] on that day, because you heard then that the Anakim are there, as well as large fortified cities. Perhaps the Lord will be with me and I will drive them out as the Lord promised."

¹³ Then Joshua blessed Caleb son of Jephunneh and gave him Hebron as an inheritance. ¹⁴ Therefore, Hebron has belonged to Caleb son of Jephunneh the Kenizzite as an inheritance to this day, because he remained loyal to the Lord, the God of Israel. ¹⁵ Hebron's name used to be Kiriath-arba; Arba was the greatest man among the Anakim. After this, the land had rest from war.

Joshua 14:6-15

LESSON 12

Principles to Live By

It's hard to stay faithful behind the scenes. Most of us function better when we know people are watching us and noticing how we're doing—a natural tendency. At times, though, the Lord Jesus wants to test our ability to perform behind the scenes while someone else garners all the attention on stage.

Caleb, a dynamic leader, models humility and faithfulness like few others. When he and Joshua, alone among the spies, supported invading Canaan, it was Caleb who spoke up first at great risk to himself (Num. 13:30; 14:10). At that time he seemed to be the stronger leader. Certainly he was Joshua's spiritual equal. God, however, chose Joshua as Moses' successor to lead Israel. Without a hint of grumbling, Caleb quietly supported God's designated leader.

God had promised Caleb that when Israel conquered Canaan, he could seize the hill country around Hebron as his family inheritance. Years passed, and more years. The invasion finally occurred. Forty-five years after God's promise, Caleb stepped forward to claim it. God honored that claim, in large part because of Caleb's strength of character shown in his patience and faithfulness

Principle 1

God honors men who courageously walk in His will.

Three times the Bible emphasizes that Caleb followed the Lord completely or loyally (Num. 14:24; Deut. 1:36, Josh. 14:14). God honored Caleb's faithful obedience both as a young spy and as an enthusiastic older man.

God wants us to be obedient in all that He asks of us. Although entry into the promised land was postponed, God viewed Caleb's *willingness to obey* as actual obedience. But despite his obedience, Israel's disobedience postponed Caleb's opportunity to enter and take the land.

There are times when family members, church folk, business colleagues, or friends limit our ability to be as responsive to the will of God as we'd like to be. God knows our hearts at those times. When circumstances beyond our control limit what we can do for God, He takes that into account.

Caleb also illustrates for us the importance of never letting go of our desire to serve the Lord in an area that He has placed on our hearts, even when we are limited by people or circumstances. People and circumstances can change, and new opportunities to fulfill an old passion implanted by God may reappear. Always be ready to go as far as you can in doing God's will at any time that God opens the door of opportunity.

PRINCIPLE 2

GOD HONORS MEN WHO TAKE A STAND AGAINST THE MAJORITY WHEN THE MAJORITY IS WRONG.

Caleb's obedience as a spy showed itself in a minority report at Kadesh-barnea. The vote among the spies was 10 to 2 in favor of disobedience.

How easy it is to side with the majority, to compromise our Christian convictions, and to operate out of fear. Not so with Caleb. Even when Joshua appeared to be reluctant to speak up as the other 10 spies grumbled about the dangers of Canaan, Caleb spoke out boldly. We need to internalize and outwardly display the same courage and conviction that Caleb possessed.

PRINCIPLE 3

GOD HONORS MEN WHO TAKE A STAND FOR HIM EVEN WHEN IT MEANS REJECTION BY THE GROUP.

Caleb obeyed God against the backdrop of group rejection. The children of Israel literally wanted to stone him (Num. 14:10). Most of us have never had our lives threatened because of our stand for God's truth and Kingship. However, it's easy to be inhibited and fearful even in the face of minor rejection by those who don't want to follow God.

The apostle Paul also stands out as a dynamic example for all of us in this respect. When he knew he was going to stand before the Roman emperor, perhaps to face the death penalty, he wrote to his faithful supporters in Philippi: "My eager expectation and hope is that I will not be ashamed about anything, but that now as always, with all boldness, Christ will be highly honored in my body, whether by life or by death" (Phil. 1:20).

PRINCIPLE 4

GOD HONORS MEN WHO FAITHFULLY FOLLOW HIM OVER THE LONG HAUL.

Caleb had obeyed and followed the Lord for 45 years, even though God had chosen Joshua to lead the children of Israel into Canaan. He could have become jealous and resentful of Joshua. He could have felt he deserved to lead as much as Joshua did. Caleb's zeal and commitment never faded although he stayed behind the scenes.

Behind-the-scenes faithfulness is never easy, but it serves as a reflection of true character. At times, God tests us to see how faithful we are under circumstances like Caleb's. If we pass the test, He is glorified and then able to entrust us with greater responsibility.

<table>
<tr><td>PRINCIPLE 5</td></tr>
</table>

GOD WILL NOT FORGET MEN WHO SERVE HIM FAITHFULLY AND CONSISTENTLY.

God eventually rewarded and honored Caleb's obedience, even though 45 years had elapsed. God never forgot His promise to Caleb. He always honors faithful obedience. As in Caleb's case, some of that reward may come to us during our lifetime. The rest will definitely await us in eternity. Eternal rewards, of course, are the best kind.

QUESTIONS FOR INTERACTION

1. If you live to be 85, what do you want to be doing then?
   a. Lying on the beach and soaking in the rays
   b. Fishing or gardening
   c. Taking on the biggest challenge of my life
   d. Writing my memoirs
   e. Other _____

2. What kind of life do you need to live now to remain optimistic and courageous into old age?

3. What past memories fueled Caleb's determination to capture Hebron (Josh. 14:6-9)?

4. What present frame of mind fueled Caleb's determination to capture Hebron (vv. 10-12)?

5. What heritage did Caleb gain and pass on because of his faithful determination (vv. 13-15)?

6. What other attributes besides physical strength can an older man use effectively in the Lord's service?

LESSON 12

7. What would you like to be remembered for accomplishing as an older man in each of these areas?
   a. Work achievements
   b. Ministry
   c. Relationships
   d. Societal impact
   e. Walk with God

GOING DEEPER

8. At age 85, Caleb could say he had "remained loyal to the LORD my God" (Josh. 14:9). Which of these statements best describes your spiritual loyalty?
   a. I sort of walk with the Lord my God.
   b. Sometimes I walk faithfully with the Lord my God.
   c. I work at walking with the Lord my God.
   d. I walk wholeheartedly with the Lord my God.
   e. Sometimes I run; sometimes I stumble.
   f. Other _____.

9. Which of these is the biggest hindrance to the consistency of your walk with God?
   a. Lack of discipline
   b. Inability to balance an over-crowded schedule
   c. A job/career that demands total loyalty
   d. A family member who opposes my spiritual commitments
   e. Uncertainty about whether I want to be really committed; a lukewarm attitude
   f. Other _____

10. What is it that truly motivates you to pursue consistency and faithfulness in your walk with God?

CARING TIME

We know of Caleb because he courageously filed a minority report in favor of invading Canaan. The majority of the spies convinced the Israelites that they could never overthrow its strongly fortified cities or defeat the giants who lived there (Num. 13–14). Just as Caleb modeled a life of courage in the face of opposition, we need to consider how we can spur one another on to this kind of gutsy manhood.

1. What opposition or ridicule do you face because you are a Christian? Where do you experience this most acutely?

2. (Ask this question of each man who responds to question 1.) How could (group member's name) respond to that opposition in ways that honor God and show love to his adversary?

3. Let's pray around the group. Each of you pray for the man to your left that he will be courageous and loving this week as he stands up for his faith and responds to opposition he may encounter.

NEXT WEEK

Next week we move to the end of the book of Joshua and listen in on Joshua's farewell speeches to the leaders and people of Israel. In chapter 23, Joshua does all the talking as he delivers his personal farewell. In chapter 24, Joshua interacts with Israel as he leads the nation in reaffirming its commitment to the Lord. It's in that context that Joshua uttered his most famous words: "Choose for yourselves today the one you will worship. … As for me and my family, we will worship the Lord" (Josh. 24:15).

SCRIPTURE NOTES

JOSHUA 14:6-15

14:6-15 Caleb son of Jephunneh. Caleb, one of the original spies sent into Canaan, revealed his lifelong plans and zeal for securing his inheritance in Hebron.

14:7 Kadesh-barnea. This oasis in the wilderness of Paran was some 70 miles south of Hebron and 150 miles north of Mount Sinai. During the second year after the exodus from Egypt, Moses sent out 12 spies from Kadesh-barnea in preparation for invading Canaan. Because Israel was afraid to invade Canaan, God forced them to wander for 40 years until that first fearful generation died off.

14:12 Anakim. The Anakim were fierce giants. It was they who had so overwhelmingly frightened 10 of the original 12 spies that they would not invade Canaan (Num. 13:33). Many of the Anakim had died in the conquest under Joshua (Josh. 11:21). Caleb relished the chance to wipe out the remaining survivors. Later, a remnant took refuge in Philistia.

14:13 Hebron. Roughly 19 miles south of Jerusalem, Hebron had been the favored city of Abraham (Gen. 13:18) and the burial place of the patriarchs (Gen. 25:9; 35:27-29; 50:13). The 12 spies had visited Hebron (Num. 13:22). Caleb's interest in the place may have sprung from that time.

14:15 Kiriath-arba. The former name of Hebron, *Kiriath* meant "city" and *Arba* was the name of its founder, one of the Anakim. *Arba* meant "four." This renowned giant may have been the fourth son of his father.

PERSONAL NOTES

DECISIVE DECISION REQUIRED

LAST WEEK

Last week we saw Caleb emerge from the background to claim a 45-year-old promise. During all those years he had faithfully served God behind the scenes while Joshua served in the limelight as God's designated leader of Israel. When it was time for the tribe of Judah to claim its inheritance, Caleb stepped forward to claim Hebron. Not surprisingly, God honored the old man of faithfulness and courage. God had never forgotten Caleb's faith and courage as one of the original spies in Canaan all those years before. God rewarded that faith and courage and particularly his ongoing faithfulness by giving his aged servant a great victory over giants in the land.

ICEBREAKER

Famous last words … President Eisenhower is quoted as saying, "I've always loved my wife, my children, and my grandchildren, and I've always loved my country. I want to go. God, take me." Lady Astor awoke from a doze to find her whole family gathered. She smiled and whispered, "Am I dying, or is it my birthday?" Humphrey Bogart reportedly said, "I should have never switched from Scotch to martinis."

1. What's the most difficult good-bye you ever had to say?

2. Does anybody in the group remember the general content of one of the following important speeches? Why or why not?
   a. Your high school or college graduation
   b. Your wedding charge
   c. Any President's inaugural address
   d. Your pastor's last sermon
   e. The last words of a godly man or woman who finished life well

3. Whose funeral that you attended was most characterized by positive remembrances of the deceased? What made that person so remarkable?

The book of Joshua ends with two speeches Joshua made to Israel before his death at the age of 110 (Josh. 24:29). The first address reminded the nation of all God had done for them and urged the people to love and serve Him. The second message was delivered at Shechem, the town in the valley between Mount Ebal and Mount Gerizim where Israel had renewed its covenant with God before the conquest of Canaan (Josh. 8:30-35). On that same site, Joshua strongly challenged Israel to take that covenant seriously.

Joshua's Charge to Remain Strong and Faithful

[1] A long time after the Lord had given Israel rest from all the enemies around them, Joshua was old, getting on in years. [2] So Joshua summoned all Israel, including its elders, leaders, judges, and officers, and said to them, … [6] "Be very strong, and continue obeying all that is written in the book of the law of Moses, so that you do not turn from it to the right or left [7] and so that you do not associate with these nations remaining among you. Do not call on the names of their gods or make an oath to them; do not worship them or bow down to them. [8] Instead, remain faithful to the Lord your God, as you have done to this day.

[9] "The Lord has driven out great and powerful nations before you, and no one has been able to stand against you to this day. [10] One of you routed a thousand, because the Lord your God was fighting for you, as He promised. [11] So be very diligent to love the Lord your God for your own well-being. [12] For if you turn away and cling to the rest of these nations remaining among you, and if you intermarry or associate with them and they with you, [13] know for certain that the Lord your God will not continue to drive these nations out before you. They will become a snare and a trap for you, a scourge for your sides and thorns in your eyes, until you disappear from this good land the Lord your God has given you."

Joshua 23:1-2a, 6-13

Joshua's Challenge to Choose Allegiances

[1] Joshua assembled all the tribes of Israel at Shechem and summoned Israel's elders, leaders, judges, and officers, and they presented themselves before God. [2] Joshua said to all the people, … [14] "Therefore, fear the Lord and worship Him in sincerity and truth. Get rid of the gods your ancestors worshiped beyond the Euphrates River and in

Egypt, and worship the Lord. ¹⁵ But if it doesn't please you to worship the Lord, choose for yourselves today the one you will worship: the gods your fathers worshiped beyond the Euphrates River, or the gods of the Amorites in whose land you are living. As for me and my family, we will worship the Lord."

¹⁶ The people replied, "We will certainly not abandon the Lord to worship other gods! ¹⁷ For the Lord our God brought us and our fathers out of the land of Egypt, the place of slavery and performed these great signs before our eyes. He also protected us all along the way we went and among all the peoples whose lands we traveled through. ¹⁸ The Lord drove out before us all the peoples, including the Amorites who lived in the land. We too will worship the Lord, because He is our God."

¹⁹ But Joshua told the people, "You will not be able to worship the Lord, because He is a holy God. He is a jealous God; He will not remove your transgressions and sins. ²⁰ If you abandon the Lord and worship foreign gods, He will turn against [you], harm you, and completely destroy you, after He has been good to you."

²¹ "No!" the people answered Joshua. "We will worship the Lord."

²² Joshua then told the people, "You are witnesses against yourselves that you yourselves have chosen to worship the Lord."

"We are witnesses," they said.

Joshua 24:1-2a, 14-22

PRINCIPLES TO LIVE BY

Joshua's two culminating messages to Israel contain the basic secret to his own success as a faithful and committed man of God. These final words reflect his personal philosophy of life as a leader in Israel. Two fundamental principles emerge that have personal applications for every 21st century Christian man, and especially for every Christian leader.

PRINCIPLE 1

WE MUST BELIEVE WITH ALL OUR HEARTS THAT GOD IS THE ONLY TRUE GOD.

Once Joshua had turned from the gods of Egypt, he never forsook the one true God. Twelve times in Joshua 23, he referred to "the Lord your God" when reviewing the successes of Israel in the land of Canaan. This demonstrated who was first and foremost in Joshua's life.

When Joshua stood before the people to say farewell, he could easily have patted himself on the back. Years before God had said, "Today I will begin to exalt you in the sight of all Israel" (Josh. 3:7). Instead he consistently and persistently credited the Lord with all of Israel's victories.

Don't misunderstand! Joshua did not disregard his own accomplishments. He knew that he was a great leader. However, he also recognized himself as a human instrument in the hands of an almighty God who utilized his talents and abilities.

Joshua persisted in his commitment to God to the end of his life. It's often easy to begin our Christian lives giving glory to God, but as we grow older and as our accomplishments increase, our natural tendency is to forget the source of our strength, our abilities, and our accomplishments. We may start honoring ourselves and begin worshiping the "god of materialism," the "god of intellectualism," or the "god of self-pride."

It isn't wrong to use the word "I" when referring to our efforts and accomplishments. But a Christian man who puts God first in his life will always reflect with honesty and true humility that it is God who is responsible for all he is and has.

PRINCIPLE 2

WE MUST LOVE GOD WITH ALL OUR HEARTS.

When God gave Moses the Ten Commandments, He said first, "Do not have other gods besides Me" (Ex. 20:3). Then He added that he would show "faithful love to a thousand generations of those who love Me and keep My commands" (Ex. 20:6). The logic presented here was that if we love God, we would serve Him. Joshua followed this sequence in his life, and continually urged the children of Israel to do the same.

Jesus told His disciples to love Him in this way: "The one who has My commands and keeps them is the one who loves Me" (John 14:21a). Loving God involves obeying with our total being—our minds, our hearts, and our souls. Obviously, our emotions are involved, but obedience often involves responding to God's will whether we feel like it or not.

Joshua loved and obeyed God with wholehearted abandon. That's why he could say to Israel, "Choose for yourselves today the one you will worship. . . . As for me and my family, *we will worship the LORD*" (Josh. 24:15). This statement was the culmination of a life lived in obedience to God's Word.

Among the last words Joshua delivered to Israel were, in essence, the first words God had spoken to him at the beginning of his career: "Be very strong, and continue obeying all that is written in the book of the law of Moses, so that you do not turn from it to the right or left" (Josh. 23:6; see

Josh. 1:7). Joshua's ministry to Israel ended as it had begun, with love for God expressed through obedience. What a legacy for this great man! What a model for us today!

QUESTIONS FOR INTERACTION

1. How would you rate your love for God?
   a. Strong
   b. Above average
   c. Average
   d. Below average
   e. Weak

2. How would you rate your obedience to God?
   a. Strong
   b. Above average
   c. Average
   d. Below average
   e. Weak

3. What did Joshua say would be the benefits of obeying the law of God (Josh. 23:6, 9-10)?

4. What did Joshua say would be the consequences of disobeying the law of God (vv. 7, 12-13)?

5. How did Joshua describe the spiritual choice Israel faced (24:14-15)?

6. How did the people explain their commitment to the Lord (vv. 16-18)?

7. Why would Joshua try to talk Israel out of its commitment to the Lord (vv. 19-20)?

8. Why would Joshua make the people of Israel their own witnesses when they insisted they wanted to serve God (vv. 21-22)?

9. Once you trusted Jesus as Savior, did you take on any obligation to obey His commands (See John 14:21)?

10. What past blessings of God has God bestowed on you and your family that should motivate you to obey Him out of gratitude?

GOING DEEPER

11. At what point in your Christian life were you most aware of feeling love for God?

12. At this point in your Christian life, how would you like your love for God to develop?
    a. A more heartfelt love
    b. A more thoughtful love
    c. A more active love
    d. A love shared more with others
    e. Other _____

13. As you grow older, how can you keep your love for God from growing stale?

CARING TIME

This is our final Caring Time as part of this study. Joshua accepted the responsibility to challenge the Israelites whom he led to pursue total commitment to the Lord. We should accept such responsibility for one another in this group. We have had a unique opportunity to speak truth into one another's lives as we've studied God's Word together and met together on a regular basis.

1. As you reflect over the entire study of Joshua, what lesson has most challenged you in your Christian life? How?

2. How can we best challenge you or encourage you to implement that particular lesson in the weeks ahead?

3. In what ways can we support you in prayer for the week ahead?

SCRIPTURE NOTES

JOSHUA 23:1-2A, 6-13

23:1-2 Joshua summoned all Israel. Sensing the end of his life was near, Joshua summoned the leaders of Israel who would be his spokespersons to the rest of the nation. His parting words focused on reviewing past accomplishments and exhorting the people to continue obeying the Lord.

23:6 Be very strong. From the lips of an aged man came the exhortation to be strong. Joshua's last words to his people were the first words God had spoken to him at the beginning of his command (Josh. 1:6).

23:12 if you ... associate with them. The temptation to compromise by entertaining trade, business, or social opportunities with the pagan peoples would be very strong for the fledgling nation. What could it hurt? Joshua spelled it out for his people just as Moses had before: "No way!" If only they had listened to this wise counsel in future generations.

JOSHUA 24:1-2A, 14-22

24:1-2a, 14-22 The credits rolling at the end of Joshua's life repeat a common theme: God alone had achieved the victory for Israel. In the context of the past, Joshua provided Israel with an ultimatum for the future. Israel must respond wholeheartedly and serve the Lord alone.

24:14 fear the LORD. No single English word conveys every aspect of the word *fear* in this phrase. The meaning includes worshipful submission, reverential awe, and obedient respect to the covenant-keeping God of Israel.

24:15 As for me ... we will worship. One man registered his vote for the supremacy of God. Although he was their leader, Joshua knew that he could not speak for Israel. The choice to serve God must be a personal decision.

24:17-18 For the Lord our God. In light of Joshua's review of Israel's history, what choice could the people make other than to serve the Lord? Of course, their self-assurance in this decision would return to haunt them in the future.

24:19 You will not be able to worship the LORD. If Joshua could have talked them out of their commitment, he would have tried. If they could not confirm their spirituality with complete certainty in the presence of the family of faith, there was little hope of sticking to it when they returned home. *jealous God.* God is only called jealous in contexts concerning idolatry. Idolatry, therefore, is like adultery. As a husband burns with possessive, protective anger when his wife deserts him for another, so God responds to His people who pursue false gods.

24:22 You are witnesses. Ancient covenant ceremonies were formal affairs that were reduced to writing and signed by outside parties as witnesses. Witnesses could later be called to testify in court if one party was charged with breaking the covenant. Joshua made Israel function as their own witnesses to their oath to serve the Lord. They would indict themselves if they were untrue to God.

Personal Notes

PERSONAL NOTES

PERSONAL NOTES

PERSONAL NOTES